The Ultimate Caribbean Quiz Book

John Gilmore

Macmillan Education
Between Towns Road, Oxford OX4 3PP
A division of Macmillan Publishers Limited
Companies and representatives throughout the world

www.macmillan-caribbean.com

ISBN 0 333 97599 5

First published 2003

Designed by Stafford and Stafford
Cover design by Stafford and Stafford

Printed and bound in Malaysia

2007 2006 2005 2004 2003
10 9 8 7 6 5 4 3 2 1

Contents

For Marita and our children,
Alex, Annabelle, and Giselle;

and for my colleagues on the
Sidney Sussex College University Challenge team, 1978-79:
John Adams, Steve Badsey, Nick Graham and David Lidington

Introduction

Many years ago, I took part in an inter-school spelling contest organised by the now long-defunct Barbados *Daily News*. We got to be on television – then still a novelty in Barbados – and our team won. Perhaps that was the beginning of my fondness for spelling contests, general knowledge competitions, quiz books and miscellaneous pieces of information in general.

Later on, when I was a student in England, I was part of a team from Sidney Sussex College, Cambridge, which appeared on the popular television quiz show *University Challenge* (a British version of the game called *College Bowl* in the USA). We won that year's contest, so we appeared on television quite a number of times over a period of several months. Young ladies wrote fan letters. Total strangers stopped me in the street to offer congratulations. One of them worked for what was still called British Rail and fulfilled one of my childhood fantasies by allowing me to drive a locomotive, even if it was only for a few yards down a siding. I came to the conclusion that there is no piece of information so bizarre or so obscure that you will not be able to find a use for it some day – even if it is only to answer a quiz question.

But where was the Caribbean in all of this? I have read innumerable quiz books and found that it is a rare one which includes as much as a single question on the Caribbean. When I worked at the regional newspaper, *Caribbean Week*, I found that the syndicated quiz which we ran on our puzzle page had nothing to do with the Caribbean. To replace it, I began to compile a regular Caribbean quiz myself. That this proved to be popular with readers has encouraged me to hope that *The Ultimate Caribbean Quiz Book* may entertain both Caribbean people – at home and abroad – and visitors to the region.

There are two pleasures to be derived from quiz books. One is that of saying 'Well, I never!' or 'Amazing!' to some novel piece of information. The other is the satisfaction of reminding yourself that you were already acquainted with some particularly obscure scrap of knowledge. If you have decided you want to read this book, it seems a fair bet that you already know quite a bit about the Caribbean – so you will find few basic questions along the lines of 'What it the capital of Jamaica?' We both know that you know that. Some of the questions are fairly tough, but anyone with a good general knowledge of the Caribbean should be able to get most of them. The perspective is mainly that of the Anglophone Caribbean, but I have tried to give a reasonable coverage of the region as a whole, and to include a wide variety of subjects.

Two final points. A quiz book is not an encyclopaedia – I can't guarantee that your own best-beloved fact about the Caribbean is included. And while every effort has been made to ensure the accuracy of the answers, we are all fallible. I will never forget the quiz book in which somebody – perhaps an over-zealous proof reader – had transformed Humbert Humbert, Nabokov's lovelorn protagonist in *Lolita* into the late US Vice-President Hubert Humphrey. If I have erred, please forgive me – and then write to me, in care of the publishers, with the correct information so that we can make sure it gets into the next edition.

Happy quizzing!

QUESTIONS

1 What's in a name?

1. New Providence is in The Bahamas – but where in the Caribbean would you find Old Providence Island?

2. Where is New Sparta?

3. Apart from being the larger of the two main islands which make up the Republic of Trinidad and Tobago, Trinidad is also the name of a city in another Caribbean country. Which one?

4. The Spanish city of Santiago de Compostela, home of a famous shrine to St James the Apostle, has given its name to many towns in the New World. One of the best known is Santiago de Cuba, which is, as the name suggests, in Cuba. But where is Santiago de los Caballeros?

5. And what is the modern name of Santiago de la Vega?

6. A village in St Vincent shares its name with a town which was established in Antigua in the 17th century but abandoned in the 19th century. The name is also that of the capital of another Caribbean country – what is it?

7. The Amerindian names of some Caribbean islands are still in popular use. Which country is often referred to as Quisqueya?

8. And which Caribbean country is sometimes called Borinquen?

9. Which Caribbean country changed its name on becoming independent in 1966?

10. English Harbour is not in England, the Scotland District is not in Scotland, and Irish Town is not in Ireland. Where are they?

2 Going to extremes

1. Which is the largest island in the Caribbean?
2. Which is the highest mountain in the Caribbean islands?
3. And which is the lowest point in the Caribbean islands?
4. Where would you find the highest point in the Kingdom of the Netherlands?
5. Everybody knows the Pitons, but neither of them is the highest mountain in St Lucia. What is?
6. Which is the easternmost island in the Caribbean?
7. Which is the largest island in the Bahamas?
8. Which Commonwealth Caribbean country has the largest population?
9. Which member of the Caribbean Community (Caricom) has the smallest population?
10. Which is the largest of the French Overseas Departments in the Caribbean?

3 And then comes...

1. What is the second largest island in the Caribbean?
2. What is the second largest island in the Republic of Cuba?
3. Which is the largest island belonging wholly to the Republic of Haiti?
4. Which is the largest of the out-islands of Guadeloupe?
5. Which was the second country in the Caribbean to become independent?
6. Which was the second of the British colonies in the Caribbean to become independent?
7. In terms of size, how does Bequia rank among the islands of the Grenadines?
8. Which of the Netherlands Antilles has the second largest population?
9. What are the two largest of Puerto Rico's off-shore islands?
10. Who was St Lucia's second winner of a Nobel Prize?

4 Just keeps rolling along

1. What is the political significance of the Courantyne River?
2. Which Caribbean capital stands on the Ozama River?
3. The River Artibonite gives its name to a political division in which Caribbean country?
4. Who popularised rafting down the Rio Grande in northern Jamaica as a tourist attraction?
5. Another watery attraction tumbles into the Caribbean Sea near Ocho Rios on Jamaica's north coast. What is it?
6. Which Caribbean island claims to have as many rivers as there are days in the year?
7. Early English settlers in one Caribbean island named their capital after an 'Indian Bridge' they found over a river. Which island was this?
8. For what is River Antoine in Grenada famous?
9. The Rabacca Dry River is not always dry – where does this make travelling a problem?
10. Why does Guadeloupe have a river which isn't a river at all?

5 Where are we?

Can you identify these famous Caribbean scenes?

5
6
8
9
PENHA
PENHA
7
10

6 Not quite the same

1. Where is Fallen Jerusalem?
2. Where and what was Sevilla La Nueva?
3. Two Caribbean towns are called after the capital of the Netherlands. Which ones?
4. Which Caribbean island has places called after the English seaside towns of Brighton, Hastings and Worthing?
5. Which mainland Caribbean country has a place called after the English town of Totnes?
6. Which British overseas territory in the Caribbean had its capital named after the southern English port of Plymouth?
7. Which Caribbean island has its capital named after the northern English seaside town of Scarborough?
8. The well-known North American city of Charleston, South Carolina, was often known in the 17th and 18th centuries as Charlestown. Which Caribbean island has a capital with the same name?
9. Where in the Caribbean would you find the towns of Basseterre and Basse-Terre?
10. Which Caribbean countries have Georgetown and George Town as their respective capitals?

7 ¡Que Bonita Bandera!

Can you identify these Caribbean flags?

8 I'll fly away...

1 Which Caribbean airport is named after a local statesman who transformed his country's economy through the famous Operation Bootstrap, but who was also well-known for his dislike of flying?

2 Killed in battle fighting for his country's independence, he wrote the words to one of the Caribbean's best-known songs. He also has an airport named after him. Who was he?

3 Where in the Caribbean will you find an airport named after the Queen of the Netherlands?

4 Which Caribbean territory, which has never belonged to the United States of America, has an airport named after a US president who never set foot on the island?

5 It takes up most of the flat land in the island, but is still only 1312 feet (400 metres) long, and is said to be the shortest landing strip in regular commercial use in the world. Where is it?

6 Which Caribbean capital has 'the Americas International Airport'?

7 Which Caribbean country has an airport called after the Amerindian name for the island?

8 The name of the Zorg-en-Hoop ('Worry and Hope') Airport might be enough to make any traveller think twice. Which Caribbean capital does it serve?

9 A famous poem by Derek Walcott includes the original name of the Grantley Adams International Airport in Barbados. What was the name of the airport?

10 Where in the Caribbean would you find a space centre used for rocket launches?

9 Sites and monuments

1 At Capá, near Utuado in central Puerto Rico, there are a large number of standing stones, some with Amerindian petroglyphs. What was the site used for?

2 Where was the first European settlement in the New World?

3 Once one of the most important British fortifications in the Caribbean, it was known as 'the Gibraltar of the West Indies.' Of which Caribbean island is it now the leading tourist attraction?

4 Where in the Caribbean would you find the stone towers of two windmills dating from about 1700, standing next to each other?

5 Which British admiral spent 17 years in Kingston, Jamaica, as a break from a much longer sojourn in Spanish Town?

6 Another British admiral is commemorated by a statue in another Caribbean capital, erected many years before the better-known statue of him in London. Who is he?

7 Built on the orders of King Henri Christophe, one of the largest historical monuments in the Caribbean stands in a remote part of northern Haiti. What is it?

8 A centuries-old weathercock in the shape of a female figure appears on a well-known brand of rum. It is the symbol of which Caribbean city?

9 What is the name of the ancient fortress which is one of the major tourist attractions in San Juan, Puerto Rico?

10 Why is 56 Hope Road, Kingston, an address famous all over the world?

10 Disasters

1. Once one of the region's most important harbours, and famous as the haunt of pirates and buccaneers, this Caribbean town was destroyed by an earthquake in 1692. Where is it?
2. What was the most significant event in the Caribbean in 1780?
3. What disease swept through the Caribbean in the 1840s and 1850s, killing many thousands of people?
4. Why was 8 May 1902 a very lucky day for Louis Auguste Ciparis in Martinique?
5. Which Caribbean capital was severely damaged by an earthquake in 1907?
6. What was the *Island Queen*, and what happened to her?
7. Whose actions brought Guyana some unwanted publicity in November 1978?
8. Why did Lloyd Lovindeer want to know if anybody had seen his dish?
9. Why are the people of Antigua and St Martin unlikely to forget the events of September 1995 ?
10. Name the Caribbean island which was devastated by a series of volcanic eruptions in 1995 to 1997.

11 Animal Geography

1. Where would you find the islands of West Dog, George Dog, and Great Dog?
2. Where in the Caribbean would you find Cat Island?
3. There are several Rat Islands in the Caribbean, but only one is home to a cultural foundation established by a Nobel Prize-winner. To which country does it belong?
4. Which group of Caribbean islands is named after crocodiles?
5. Where is the Dragon's Mouth?
6. Which Caribbean islands are named after turtles?
7. Which Caribbean island has an offshore island called Hog Island, which is well-known as a picnic spot?
8. Where in the Caribbean would you find two sets of Aves Islands (which take their name from the Spanish for 'birds')?
9. There are still Pelican Islands in different parts of the Caribbean, but one Pelican Island no longer exists, having been joined to a larger island nearby when its deep-water harbour was built. Name the larger island.
10. Where has a Pigeon Island, once famous in naval and military history, been joined to the mainland?

12 All manner of four-footed beasts

1. Name the unfortunate marsupial found in some of the southern Caribbean islands which is hunted for its meat, alleged to have aphrodisiac qualities.
2. What is a tatou, and where are you most likely to see one?
3. Which is the only species of land tortoise native to the Caribbean?
4. What is 'mountain chicken'?
5. Guadeloupe is home to a mammal thought to be extinct elsewhere in the Caribbean. Can you name the animal?
6. Where would you find the world's only jaguar reserve?
7. The Caribbean is home to two species of monkey which were originally from West Africa. In which islands are they found?
8. Which Caribbean island is the home of the blackbelly sheep?
9. Which animal was imported into the Caribbean from India in the later 19th century as a means of controlling rats and snakes?
10. Barbados imported this desert animal as a beast of burden in the 17th century. Name the animal.

13 Creeping and crawling things

1 What is a wood-slave?

2 Where would you find the world's smallest snake?

3 Why might you want to put a centipede into a bottle of rum?

4 What is a fourmi-tac?

5 Which is the only Caribbean snake which presents a real hazard to man?

6 The world's longest insect, some believe its presence in a house is an omen of death, though it is in fact harmless to man. What is it?

7 In parts of the Caribbean, different kinds of lizard are called mabouya, but what is the origin of the name?

8 Why is the iguana much less common than it used to be?

9 What is a chigger?

10 Which island once possessed a railway of such remarkable slowness that some claimed it fell under the biblical condemnation that 'every creeping thing that creepeth upon the earth shall be an abomination'?

14 Feathered friends

1 Where would you find the largest nesting colony in the world of the Magnificent Frigate Bird?

2 What is a patu?

3 Where in the Caribbean would you find Birds of Paradise?

4 What's fishy about the bird that appears on the coat of arms of the University of the West Indies?

5 One southern Caribbean island calls its airport after the bird which is one of its most spectacular tourist attractions. Which island, and what is the bird?

6 Which three eastern Caribbean islands have adopted endangered species of parrot as their national bird?

7 A small white heron from Africa is now one of the most widespread birds in the Caribbean, but it was first reported in the region as recently as 1933. What is it?

8 In Bequia, which bird is supposed to call 'Bequia sweet, sweet, sweet!'?

9 Trinidad is often referred to as 'the Land of the Hummingbird', but its most spectacular bird inhabitant is somewhat larger. What is it?

10 Which island is home to the world's smallest hummingbird?

15 Creatures of the sea and river

1. Name the fish of which it is said that, if you eat it, you will some day return to Trinidad.
2. Which island is known as 'the Land of the Flying Fish'?
3. What is a blackfish?
4. What do people in the Caribbean call a dolphin?
5. What is the largest marine creature found in the Caribbean?
6. What is a sea-cat?
7. What melancholy distinction is suffered by the Kemps Ridley turtle?
8. What is the probable origin of stories about mermaids?
9. What creature appears as the crest of the Jamaican coat of arms?
10. Have you ever seen a Caribbean Monk Seal?

16 Fruits of the earth

1. What is the origin of the grapefruit?
2. How did the breadfruit come to the Caribbean?
3. Where does the world's most expensive coffee come from?
4. Which Caribbean island is particularly known for its production of nutmeg?
5. What is an Antigua Black?
6. What was Jamaica pepper?
7. Where is an ackee not an ackee?
8. What was Trinidad's most important crop in the early 20th century, with its exports averaging double the value of sugar?
9. What is Buxton Spice?
10. Which eastern Caribbean islands are important producers of bananas?

17 Pleasures of the table

1 Where would you be most likely to be offered ackee and salt-fish for breakfast?

2 For what is Boston Bay in Jamaica famous?

3 What is the essential ingredient in pepperpot, which turns a collection of scraps of almost any old meat into a tender and mouth-watering dish?

4 Why are you supposed not to talk when pudding is being cooked (for pudding and souse)?

5 One of the Caribbean's favourite fast foods, it is perhaps India's greatest contribution to the region's cooking. What is it?

6 What is mannish water?

7 What delicacy is associated with Independence time in Barbados?

8 What does an Antiguan call what a Bajan calls coucou?

9 In Trinidad and Tobago, what would you expect to find in callaloo soup?

10 Traditionally regarded as a food for children and invalids because it is so digestible, it found new uses in the manufacture of special coatings for computer paper. St Vincent is one of its major producers. What is it?

18 I'll drink to that!

1 'A hott hellish and terrible liquor' was a mid-17th-century description of what is now one of the Caribbean's favourite drinks. What is it?

2 Which was the first Caribbean island to develop the manufacture of rum?

3 What, as far as the French are concerned, is the difference between *rhum agricole* and *rhum industriel*?

4 What is *clairin*?

5 'One of sour, two of sweet, three of strong, and four of weak' make what?

6 Which Caribbean island has given its name to a well-known liqueur?

7 Which Caribbean island makes a drink distilled from cactus juice and flavoured with aniseed?

8 In the 18th century, many Caribbean people suffered from 'the dry belly ache'. Were they right in ascribing this to too much rum?

9 What was sangaree?

10 Which Spanish-sounding aunt gave her name to a liqueur now known around the world?

19 The sporting life

1. Which sport has the largest number of players and supporters in the Caribbean?

2. Who held the world chess championship from 1921 to 1927, hardly ever losing a game during this period?

3. Who became the undisputed world champion in draughts (checkers) in 1994?

4. Who was the first Caribbean athlete to win an Olympic gold medal?

5. Name the Caribbean boxer who won the gold medal in the heavyweight division at three successive Olympics.

6. Who was the Caribbean swimmer who surprised everybody by winning the 100 metres butterfly at the Seoul Olympics in 1988, setting a new Olympic record in the process?

7. Name the Guadeloupean athlete known as 'La Gazelle', who won the Olympic gold medal for France in the Women's 400 metres at Barcelona in 1992, and who won both the 400 and 200 metres at the Atlanta Olympics in 1996, but who is perhaps best remembered for her sudden departure from the Sydney Olympics in 2000.

8. Who won the gold medal in the men's high jump at the Barcelona Olympics in 1992 and went on to set a new world record the following year?

9. Who finally overcame her nickname of 'The Bronze Queen' by winning a gold medal in the 200 metres at the World Track and Field Championships in Stuttgart in 1993?

10. What major sporting venue in Trinidad moved its home in 1994 after more than a century?

20 Cricket, lovely cricket

1. Which famous English novel, published in 1837, includes a well-known mention of a cricket match in the West Indies – 'sun so hot, bat in blisters, ball scorched brown'?
2. When was the first cricket match between teams representing two different territories in the West Indies?
3. In what year did an English cricket team first tour the West Indies?
4. When was a team to represent the whole West Indies first picked to play a visiting English side?
5. In what year did a West Indies team first tour England?
6. When was the West Indies cricket team recognised as having Test status?
7. When was the first ever Test victory for the West Indies?
8. Who were 'the Spin Twins'?
9. Name 'the Three Ws'.
10. How long did Sir Garfield Sobers' record for the highest Test innings stand before it was beaten?

21 Famous Faces

Our photos show ten famous Caribbean people. How many of them can you name?

22 Go girl!

1 An important leader among the Amerindians in Hispaniola, she was hanged by the Spanish in 1503 on trumped up charges of plotting a rebellion. Today she is revered in the Dominican Republic as a national heroine. What was her nam

2 A national heroine of Jamaica, she was a leader of the Maroons in the early 18th century and many legends tell of her magical powers and skills as a strategist in guerrilla warfare. Who was she?

3 A slave on Simmons Plantation helped to inspire the 1816 Rebellion in Barbados. She said she had read in the newspapers that the slaves were to be freed, but that they would have to fight for it, 'and the way they were to do it was to set fire, as that was the way they did it in St Domingo'. Can you name her?

4 Now officially a national heroine of Barbados, she kept the small local Methodist community together in the face of persecution for two years after their chapel was destroyed by rioters in 1823 and the Methodist missionary driven out of the island. What was her name?

5 Among her most famous works is the sculpture *Negro Aroused*, (1935), which soon became a symbol of growing Caribbean nationalism. Who was she?

6 Name the founder of the Little Carib Theatre in Trinidad, whose pioneering work with traditional Caribbean dance helped to secure international recognition for this aspect of the region's heritage.

7 Name the writer and performer whose *Jamaica Labrish* and other collections emphasised the importance of Jamaican folk culture.

8 Who was the first woman to become governor of a Commonwealth country?

9 Who was the first woman to become prime minister of a Commonwealth Caribbean country?

10 Which governor general of a Commonwealth Caribbean country was a former president of the World Council of Churches, a former president of the World YWCA, and a member of the Commonwealth Eminent Persons Group on Southern Africa, whose 1986 report helped to stimulate the changes leading to a democratic South Africa?

23 Let us now praise famous men

1 In the early 16th century, what famous comment was made by the Amerindian chieftain Hatuey, when he was about to be burnt at the stake by the Spanish?

2 Who led the Black Caribs of St Vincent in their resistance against the British until he was killed in battle in 1795?

3 Who was the free-coloured landowner who led a rebellion against British rule in Grenada in 1795?

4 Most illustrious of the Caribbean's black revolutionary leaders, his death in captivity far from his beloved Haiti inspired a famous sonnet by Wordsworth. Who was he?

5 Name the leader of the 1816 slave rebellion in Barbados who is now recognised as a national hero in that country.

6 A deacon in the Baptist Church, he was the leader of the great revolt against slavery which broke out in Jamaica just after Christmas 1831. What was his name?

7 Who were Duarte, Sánchez and Mella?

8 Who came down from Stony Gut to Morant Bay in Jamaica on 11 October 1865 with 400 followers and burnt down the court house?

9 Who was the general-in-chief of the Army of Liberation during Cuba's final struggle against Spanish colonial rule, 1895-98?

10 Who was the Jamaican-born founder of the Universal Negro Improvement Association whose campaign of 'Africa for the Africans, at home and abroad', won millions of supporters in different parts of the world?

24 Servants of the people

1. Who was the first and only prime minister of the Federation of the West Indies?

2. Who ensured that 'One from ten leaves nought' was politically, if not mathematically, correct?

3. Which former Caribbean prime minister was famous for his interest in unidentified flying objects (UFOs)?

4. Name three Commonwealth Caribbean prime ministers who were the sons of politicians who had previously headed the governments of their respective countries.

5. How many Commonwealth Caribbean countries have presidents as their heads of state?

6. Which former prime minister of a Commonwealth Caribbean country is of Lebanese descent?

7. What do Edward Seaga, Lester Bird and John Compton have in common?

8. Who was the first Commonwealth Caribbean prime minister to lose a vote of confidence in his country's parliament?

9. Who is the only Commonwealth Caribbean prime minister to have been assassinated?

10. Who was the first democratically elected leader of Haiti?

25 A dangerous sort of people called pirates

1 What was the difference between a privateer and a pirate?

2 First published in Dutch in 1678, it was soon translated into other languages and became an international best-seller, giving pirates the image of bloodthirsty glamour they enjoy to this day. It remains an important source for this aspect of Caribbean history. Can you name the book?

3 Who was the pirate, notorious for his cruelties and hatred of the Spanish, who sacked the town of Maracaibo in Venezuela in 1668?

4 A pirate who turned respectable and eventually became Lieutenant-Governor of Jamaica, he was celebrated for capturing the city of Panama from the Spanish in 1671. Who was he?

5 Who were the two women who sailed with the pirate Captain Jack Rackham, alias Calico Jack, and who were themselves condemned to death for piracy in Jamaica in 1720?

6 A respectable planter in Barbados, he is said to have become a pirate in order to escape a nagging wife. But the cure was perhaps worse than the disease, for he was hanged in Charleston, South Carolina, in 1718. Can you name him?

7 Who was Blackbeard?

8 Where is 'Blackbeard's Castle' now a hotel and an important tourist attraction?

9 Which Caribbean island has a 'castle' (now a hotel) where a 19th century 'pirate' is said to have lured ships on to the nearby reefs by hanging lanterns in the coconut trees?

10 Which Caribbean country used to have an official seal with a motto referring to the expulsion of the pirates and the restoration of legitimate trade?

26 Want the doctor help with that?

1 Which Caribbean country voted in 1995 to replace one medical doctor with another as its prime minister?

2 Where did a dentist become president in 1992, returning to head his country's government after 28 years in opposition?

3 Who were Papa Doc and Baby Doc?

4 Which Caribbean prime minister was frequently referred to as 'the Doctor', though he was not a medical man, but a distinguished historian with the degree of Doctor of Philosophy?

5 What is the national bird of Jamaica?

6 What, in meteorological terms, is 'the Doctor'?

7 What is a bush-doctor?

8 What is the traditional name in many parts of the English-speaking Caribbean for a druggist's or pharmacist's premises?

9 Where would you find Doctor's Cove Beach, an important tourist attraction for nearly a century?

10 Can you complete this rhyme about a famous 18th century physician who was born in the Caribbean?

I, John Lettsom,
Blisters, bleeds and sweats 'em.
If, after that, they please to die,
'..'

27 Money makes the world go around

1. How many different kinds of dollar are in use in the Caribbean?
2. Which British territories in the Caribbean use the US dollar as their official currency?
3. Which Caribbean currency has the highest value in relation to the US dollar?
4. How many countries use the Eastern Caribbean (EC) dollar?
5. Where would you find pesos in use in the Caribbean?
6. Where in the Caribbean would you find the ordinary coins and notes of a European country in circulation as the official currency?
7. Which European unit of currency has given its name to three different Caribbean currencies?
8. In which Caribbean Basin countries is the unit of currency named after famous people?
9. In the English colonies in the 17th century, there were few coins in circulation. What did people often use for money instead?
10. What was the 'piece of eight' famous in pirate stories?

28 First peoples

1. What do 'canoe,' 'hammock' and 'hurricane' have in common?
2. What was the principal crop cultivated by the Amerindians throughout the Caribbean islands?
3. What was guanín?
4. What was – or is – a bohío?
5. How did the Amerindians make their canoes?
6. What was a zemi?
7. Which Amerindian habit has been most widely adopted by other peoples?
8. What was the importance of the conch shell to the indigenous peoples of the Caribbean?
9. Which Amerindian word has given its name to a political concept in modern Latin America?
10. Where do descendants of the original inhabitants of the Caribbean still live?

29 Principalities and powers

1 Which Caribbean town is named after a king of Sweden?

2 The name of Tumble Down Dick Bay in St Eustatius is said to be a derisive reference to the brief reign of a European ruler. Who was he?

3 King of Great Britain at the time of his country's abolition of slavery in its colonies, he saw service in the Royal Navy in the Caribbean in the later 18th century, before he came to the throne. The story of his encounter with a Bridgetown hotel keeper called Rachel Pringle is still told to tourists in Barbados. Who was he?

4 Having proclaimed himself Emperor of his country, he refused to reward his followers by creating noble titles for them, allegedly saying, 'Moi seul, je suis noble'. Can you name him?

5 Which Caribbean ruler is said to have committed suicide by shooting himself with a silver bullet?

6 Who was the second person to claim the title of Emperor of Haiti?

7 Which Caribbean church saw the coronation of three Kings of the Mosquitoes in the first half of the 19th century?

8 Where in the Caribbean will you find the tomb of one of the last descendants of the last Byzantine Emperor of Constantinople?

9 A Caribbean island claims to have given two empresses to Europe. Which island? And who were the empresses?

10 A portrait of Franz Josef, Emperor of Austria from 1848 to 1916, appears on the label of an internationally famous Caribbean product. What is the product, and what has the Emperor got to do with it?

30 Curiosities of colonialism

1. Which island moved back and forth between the Windwards and the Leewards?
2. Which islands once formed the Danish West Indies?
3. Two Caribbean islands are each shared by more than one country. Which ones?
4. What are the remaining British Overseas Territories in the Caribbean?
5. Which is the only Caribbean country which has ever conquered and annexed another Caribbean country?
6. Only one Caribbean country has ever voluntarily returned to the rule of the former colonial power after independence. Which one?
7. Which Caribbean island was once the subject of several attempts at settlement by colonists from what is now Latvia?
8. Which island was the only Swedish colony in Caribbean history?
9. Which were the last Spanish colonies in the Caribbean?
10. Which Caribbean territory changed hands the most times among the different colonial powers?

31 Africa and the Caribbean

1 Why has the island of Gorée off the coast of Senegal become a tourist attraction of a peculiarly grim kind?

2 What was the approximate duration of the slave trade to the Caribbean?

3 Enslaved as a child in West Africa and taken to the Caribbean and then North America, he later obtained his freedom and became a well-known figure in the anti-slavery movement in Britain. He wrote a famous autobiography which includes a rare account of the slave trade from the point of view of one of its victims. Can you name him?

4 Born in St Thomas in the Danish West Indies in 1832, he later migrated to Liberia, where he filled a number of important posts, including that of Liberian ambassador to Britain. Can you name this major figure in the development of Pan-Africanism, who wrote a number of influential books, including *Christianity, Islam and the Negro Race?*

5 Name the Barbadian poet who lived in Ghana for eight years and whose work has been a major influence in encouraging writers in the English-speaking Caribbean to explore their African heritage.

6 What does a Jamaican mean by 'unu' or a Bajan by 'wunnah'?

7 One of the world's most ancient board games, it was brought from Africa to the Caribbean, where it is still popular in Antigua and, to a lesser extent, Barbados. What is it called?

8 What is a susu or meeting?

9 Who was Milton King?

10 Why does the flag of Ghana incorporate a black star?

32 Vive la France!

1. Name the three Overseas Departments of France in the Caribbean.

2. Which is the largest of the former French colonies in the region?

3. A famous 18th century naval encounter was called the Battle of the Saints. What were – or are – the Saints?

4. Why are the Iles du Salut (Salvation Islands or Safety Islands) perhaps inappropriately named?

5. Which is the only Commonwealth Caribbean country whose legal system is based to a significant extent on French law?

6. Which Caribbean island was for much of the 17th century shared by the English and the French, with the French taking the two ends and the English the middle?

7. In French history, who occupies a position similar to that of William Wilberforce in Britain?

8. Born in Cayenne in Guyane (French Guiana), he was the first black colonial governor in French history. In 1940 as Governor of Tchad, he was the first colonial governor to rally to General de Gaulle's Free French, and later became Governor General of French Equatorial Africa. Who was he?

9. Name the French poet and diplomat, born in Guadeloupe, who was awarded the Nobel Prize for Literature in 1960.

10. Name the Martiniquan poet who was a co-founder of the Négritude movement and for half a century was mayor of Fort-de-France.

33 Let's go Dutch

1. Which two Caribbean islands have capitals with the same name?
2. Which two Caribbean capitals are sometimes referred to locally by the same nickname?
3. What are the three self-governing partners which form the Kingdom of the Netherlands?
4. How many territories are included in the Netherlands Antilles?
5. When did Aruba leave the Netherlands Antilles?
6. What is the official name of the island popularly referred to as Statia?
7. In 1667, when the Dutch were ceded Suriname (until then an English colony), what did they give the English instead?
8. When did Suriname become independent?
9. Apart from Suriname, what other territories on the South American mainland were once Dutch colonies?
10. From the Dutch point of view, which are the Leeward Islands and which the Windward?

34 The American connection

1 From where did the Reverend Samuel Parris bring the slave Tituba to Salem, Massachusetts?

2 Which is the only place outside the present United States ever visited by George Washington?

3 Who is the only person born in the Caribbean to appear on the currency of the United States?

4 Where was an American flag being flown by a United States naval vessel first saluted by officials of a foreign power?

5 Which Caribbean capital has one of its main avenues named after John Brown, the Abolitionist?

6 What were the main results of the Spanish-American War of 1898?

7 Where in the Caribbean does the United States maintain a naval base on territory disputed with the host country?

8 What is Puerto Rico's present relationship to the United States?

9 In the words of Sparrow's calypso, what had 'the mother and the daughter working for the Yankee dollar' during the Second World War?

10 There is a small uninhabited island to the west of Haiti which is US territory. What is it called?

35 Asia and the Caribbean

1 How long did the system of bringing indentured labourers from India to the British Caribbean last?

2 Approximately how many Indians came to Trinidad and Guyana as indentured labourers during this period?

3 What was the *Fatel Rozach*?

4 Apart from Trinidad and Guyana, which other Caribbean territories have significant communities of Indian descent?

5 Which Asian countries, besides India, have had significant migration to the Caribbean?

6 Originally brought to the Caribbean by Indian immigrants, this Muslim religious festival in honour of two grandchildren of the Prophet Mohammed survives in Trinidad and (to a lesser extent) Jamaica in a thoroughly Caribbeanised form. What is it called?

7 What is chutney, when it is not something to eat?

8 What is the Arabic name commonly used to refer to the pilgrimage to Mecca which every Muslim hopes to make at least once in his or her lifetime?

9 When and where might you encounter abeer?

10 What is Divali?

36 The sweet negotiation of sugar

1 What is the original home of the sugar-cane?

2 What is the sugar-cane's scientific name?

3 How did sugar-cane reach the Caribbean?

4 In Caribbean history, what was the Sugar Revolution?

5 What were cane-holes?

6 When was the first attempt to apply steam power to the crushing of canes?

7 Why did the introduction of the vacuum pan make such a difference to the sugar industry?

8 Who first recognised sugar-cane seedlings?

9 Why do Caribbean people have good reason to remember the name of Franz Carl Achard?

10 Which country is the Caribbean's largest producer of sugar?

37 Cultural miscellany

1 What is a Moko Jumbie?

2 From Jamaica to Curaçao, he is one of the most popular figures in Caribbean folklore. A born trickster, he can change his shape at will, but he usually appears in the form of a spider. Can you name him?

3 What caused the Canboulay Riots in Port of Spain in 1881?

4 What cultural change was marked by Norman LeBlanc singing *Jerningham the Governor* in 1898?

5 Which eastern Caribbean country celebrates a festival based on the end of the sugar-cane harvest?

6 Whose funeral takes place on Ash Wednesday every year in Martinique?

7 Which country celebrates its Junkanoo Festival at Christmas and New Year?

8 Name the calypso which became a major hit for the American group, the Andrews Sisters, in 1944, and which became the subject of an important copyright lawsuit in 1946-47. Who was the original composer?

9 Name the members of the original Wailers.

10 Who designed the opening pageant for the 1992 Olympic Games in Barcelona?

38 Many mansions

1. Who was Yocahu?

2. An enormous modern statue in Santo Domingo commemorates the Dominican friar who, in a sermon preached the Sunday before Christmas 1511, was the first to denounce the cruelties the Spanish were inflicting on the indigenous peoples of the Caribbean. Who was he?

3. Who was the Dominican friar who made important contributions to the early history and anthropology of the Americas, but who is best known for his zeal for the conversion of the Amerindians and for his attempts to protect them from the abuses of the Spanish colonisers?

4. Which religious group first sent missionaries to the Caribbean for the express purpose of converting the enslaved Africans?

5. Who was Nathaniel Gilbert?

6. How did the Baptist Church come to Jamaica?

7. The Anglican Church has existed in the Caribbean since the 17th century, but when did it get its first bishops?

8. Who is the Yoruba god of thunder who gives his name to a religious cult in Trinidad?

9. In Haitian vodun, who is the guardian of the crossroads who is often invoked at the beginning of ceremonies?

10. How does Rastafarianism get its name?

39 Godliness and good learning

1 Which was the first university to be established in the Americas?

2 Where would you find the oldest theological college in the Anglican communion?

3 What was the Lady Mico Charity?

4 What was the Rawle Institute?

5 Can you name the director of education in Trinidad and Tobago who compiled the *Nelson's West Indian Readers*, familiar to generations of schoolchildren in the Anglophone Caribbean?

6 And can you name the famous calypso by Sparrow which mocked the same Readers?

7 When was the University of the West Indies established?

8 The second campus of the University of the West Indies was established at St Augustine in Trinidad in 1961, but incorporated a much older institution. Which one?

9 How old is the Barbados campus of the University of the West Indies?

10 When was the Caribbean Examinations Council established?

40 I was glad...

1 Where would you find the oldest Christian cathedral in the Americas?

2 Where is the oldest Anglican cathedral outside the British Isles?

3 Which building in the Caribbean is claimed to be the largest wooden church in the world?

4 Where would you find the oldest synagogue in continuous use in the Americas?

5 Which Caribbean capital is said to be the only place in the world where you will find a synagogue and a mosque standing next to each other?

6 In which Caribbean capital will you find an Anglican cathedral, a Roman Catholic cathedral, and a Methodist church next to each other?

7 The decoration of which church building played a major role in drawing international attention to a now world-renowned Caribbean art form?

8 Which St Lucian artist is famous for his murals in churches?

9 Which Caribbean cathedral was designed by the man who built the Eiffel Tower in Paris?

10 Which Caribbean church is famous for the story of the moving coffins in a vault in the churchyard?

41 Art and artists

1 An Italian painter who lived and worked in the Caribbean in the 1770s, he is well known for his depictions of Carib life in Dominica and St Vincent, as well as for his pictures of slave and free-coloured life in the islands. Can you name him?

2 Who was the medical doctor from the Virgin Islands who designed the Capitol of the United States of America in Washington DC?

3 One of the best known of early Caribbean artists, he achieved some recognition in Europe in the 1840s, but has only been rediscovered in his native Trinidad in recent years. Who was he?

4 Who was the major French impressionist painter born in St Thomas, in what were still the Danish West Indies?

5 And which famous French painter lived for a while in Martinique in 1887, before going on to settle in French Polynesia?

6 Name the Cuban painter who was a friend of Picasso and who himself became famous for his 'Neo-African' impressionist paintings.

7 A painter and sculptor who is perhaps the most famous of Jamaica's self-taught artists, he was also the Bishop of a Revivalist group. What was the name by which he was best known?

8 Who is the Guyanese abstract artist whose works include a series of paintings inspired by the music of Shostakovich?

9 Can you name the sculptor whose best known work is a larger than life-size statue, *Slave in Revolt*, commissioned by the Government of Barbados to mark the 150th anniversary of Emancipation?

10 Who produced the controversial statue of Bob Marley which is now in the National Gallery of Jamaica?

42 Also known as...

Can you give the real names of the following well-known figures in Caribbean music?

1 Arrow

2 Sparrow

3 Kitchener

4 Black Stalin

5 Roaring Lion

6 Gypsy

7 SuperBlue

8 Garnet Silk

9 The Mighty Gabby

10 Red Plastic Bag

43 Music, maestro!

Which Caribbean countries are particularly associated with the following forms of music and dance?

1 Reggae

2 Calypso

3 Merengue

4 Tumba

5 Zouk

6 Tuk

7 Mento

8 Bachata

9 Salsa

10 Parang

44 Talk yuh talk!

1 Which language has the second largest number of speakers in the Caribbean?

2 What do people speak in Aruba, Bonaire and Curaçao?

3 What is Sranan Tongo?

4 How many languages are in common use in St Martin/Sint Maarten?

5 What are the main Asian languages found in the Caribbean?

6 Which Caribbean territories have French as their official language?

7 Where in the Caribbean was a Dutch-based creole once in common use?

8 One major Caribbean island was never a French colony, yet the French influence was so strong that for a century most of the population spoke French or French creole. Which island?

9 In which Caribbean islands which have English as their official language is French creole the common speech of the people?

10 Which Caribbean territory has Spanish and English as its official languages?

45 More in the mortar...

Proverbs are a well-loved expression of folk wisdom throughout the Caribbean, and many are familiar around the region, with only slight variations. Can you complete these well-known examples?

1 Play wid puppy...

2 Empty bag...

3 What sweet in goat mout'...

4 Parson christen...

5 Stone a' river-bottom...

6 Every skin-teet'...

7 Two man rat...

8 Duppy know...

9 Yuh can hide an' buy ground...

10 De higher monkey climb...

46 Songs my mother taught me

1. Which country gave us the tune known in much of the Caribbean as *Yellow Bird*?
2. What claim was made by the main character in the song *Murder in de Market*?
3. What did Sammy plant down the gully?
4. What did the singer of *Linstead Market* find would not sell?
5. In a singing game popular all over the English-speaking Caribbean, who is it who is 'in the ring' and of whom we are told 'I love sugar, an' she love plum'?
6. Did Millie go to Brazil?
7. Of whom is it sung 'Ask him what de time is, Him look pon de sun'?
8. Who was King Ja Ja?
9. What did 'sly mongoose' do with the big fat chicken?
10. Originally a fishermen's song from the Bahamas, it became popular as a spiritual in the American South, and is now well known in many parts of the world. Can you name it?

47 The Fourth Estate

Which Caribbean countries are home to the following newspapers?

1 *Daily Gleaner*

2 *Advocate*

3 *Granma*

4 *Listín Diario*

5 *Stabroek News*

6 *De Ware Tijd*

7 *The Labour Spokesman*

8 *Outlet*

9 *France-Antilles*

10 *The Crusader*

48 Where did I read about them?

1 Who was 'the white witch of Rose Hall'?

2 Who successfully massaged himself into G. Ramsay Muir, Esq, MBE?

3 One of London's best known West Indians was looking forward to some decent sleep at last, but he got a nasty shock when he learnt that Aunty was coming to stay. Why?

4 Who asked 'Do angels wear brassieres?' And what was the answer?

5 Which major figure in Caribbean history has been the subject of plays by both Derek Walcott and Aimé Césaire?

6 What was the name of the family whose story is told inthe best-selling *Kaywana* trilogy by the Guyanese author Edgar Mittelholzer?

7 One of everybody's favourite aunts, but you might think twice about taking her to a cricket match. Can you name this famous creation of Trinidadian poet and storyteller Paul Keens-Douglas?

8 Who wanted to ask Kaiser and Jaillin to his birthday party? And why was he not surprised when his mother refused?

9 What was the name of the Amerindian cacique who led a rebellion against Spanish rule in early 16th century Hispaniola, preserving his people's independence until his death, and who is commemorated in the most famous novel in the literature of the Dominican Republic?

10 Who was 'the Robespierre of the Americas' who ruled Guadeloupe during the period of the French Revolution, and who is perhaps best known through his fictionalised appearance in a novel by the Cuban writer Alejo Carpentier?

49 Literary ladies

1 Wife of an early 19th century governor of Jamaica, her journal provides a fascinating picture of the planter society of the day. Who was she?

2 Born in Bermuda, she was a slave there, in the Turks Islands and in Antigua, before escaping to England and becoming the first black woman in Britain to publish an autobiographical narrative. Can you name her?

3 A nurse in Jamaica, in Central America and in the Crimean War (1853-56), she has a hall of residence at the Mona Campus of the University of the West Indies named after her. Who was she and what was the title of her book?

4 After writing a number of fairly successful novels, she disappeared from the literary scene for nearly 30 years, before resurfacing with a novel which returned to her West Indian roots and brought her international acclaim. What is the name by which she is best known?

5 Who was the Minister of Labour and Social Affairs in the government of the Federation of the West Indies? She achieved perhaps greater fame as the author of a novel which was made into a successful television series.

6 Born Elaine Potter Richardson in Antigua, she became famous as the author of a collection of sketches of Caribbean childhood called *At the Bottom of the River*. She has written several novels and other works since. What name does she write under?

7 Name the Belizean writer famous for her novel of a convent schoolgirl's growth to maturity.

8 Who won the first Commonwealth Writers' Prize in 1987 for her collection of prose fiction, *Summer Lightning and other stories*?

9 Name the Guyanese writer whose *i is a long memoried woman* won the 1983 Commonwealth Poetry Prize.

10 Who is the Guadeloupean writer of *Segou*, a two-part epic novel of African history which was a bestseller in France?

50 Author, author!

Match the titles of these well-known works of Caribbean literature to their authors. (Which country does each author come from?)

1	*Mother Poem*	a	V. S. Naipaul
2	*The Kingdom of This World*	b	Aimé Césaire
3	*Stories written in Exile*	c	Jean Rhys
4	*Return to my Native Land*	d	Joseph Zobel
5	*In the Castle of My Skin*	e	Jacques Roumain
6	*Wide Sargasso Sea*	f	Kamau Brathwaite
7	*Another Life*	g	Alejo Carpentier
8	*West Indies Ltd*	h	Juan Bosch
9	*Masters of the Dew*	i	George Lamming
10	*A House for Mr Biswas*	j	Nicolás Guillén
11	*Black Shack Alley*	k	Derek Walcott

ANSWERS

1 What's in a name?

1. Now generally known as Providencia, Old Providence Island lies in the Western Caribbean. With its sister island of San Andrés, it forms part of the territory of the Republic of Colombia.
2. New Sparta (in Spanish, Nueva Esparta) is the Venezuelan state which consists of the islands of Margarita, Coche and Cubagua. New Sparta received the name as a tribute to the bravery of the inhabitants in the War of Independence against the Spanish.
3. The city of Trinidad, renowned for its fine colonial architecture, is in Cuba.
4. Santiago de los Caballeros (St James of the Knights) is the second largest city of the Dominican Republic.
5. Santiago de la Vega (St James of the Plain) is now known as Spanish Town, Jamaica. The old name (or its English variant, St Jago de la Vega) continued in occasional use until the early 19th century.
6. Bridgetown.
7. The Dominican Republic is often referred to as Quisqueya, and its inhabitants as Quisqueyanos, after the name of one of the main Amerindian peoples living there at the time of Columbus's arrival.
8. Borinquen is an Amerindian name sometimes used for Puerto Rico.
9. British Guiana changed its name to Guyana on becoming independent in 1966.
10. English Harbour is in Antigua, the Scotland District is in Barbados, and Irish Town is in Jamaica. There was also a village called Irishtown in Barbados, which seems to have disappeared as a result of the 1898 hurricane.

2 Going to extremes

1. Cuba is the largest island in the Caribbean.
2. The highest mountain in the Caribbean islands – rising to over 10400 feet (3175 metres) above sea level – is Pico Duarte in the Dominican Republic.
3. Lago Enriquillo, also in the Dominican Republic, is the lowest point in the Caribbean islands. It is 150 feet (40 metres) below sea level.
4. In the Netherlands Antilles: it is the top of Mount Scenery in Saba, which is nearly 3000 feet (870 metres) above sea level.
5. Morne Gimie, which reaches over 3100 feet (nearly 950 metres), is the highest mountain in St Lucia.
6. Barbados is the easternmost island in the Caribbean.
7. Andros is the largest island in the Bahamas.
8. Jamaica has the largest population of any Commonwealth Caribbean country (about 2.5 million).
9. Montserrat is the Caricom member with the smallest population – approximately 11000 before the volcanic eruptions of 1995 to 1997. These led to substantial emigration, causing the population to fall to about 3000, though more recently many Montserratians have returned to the island.
10. French Guiana (Guyane) is the largest of the French Overseas Departments in the Caribbean. It is approximately 35 000 square miles, or a little under 90 000 square kilometres – about one-sixth the size of France.

3 And then comes...

1 Hispaniola, shared by Haiti and the Dominican Republic, is the second largest island in the Caribbean.

2 After Cuba itself, the second largest island is the Isla de la Juventud (Isle of Youth), formerly known as the Isla de las Pinos (Isle of Pines). It is 857 square miles (2220 square kilometres) in area, or rather less than half the size of Trinidad.

3 The Ile de la Gonâve, which is about 250 square miles (648 square kilometres) in area, or nearly the size of Dominica. Haiti itself is only the western third or so of the island of Hispaniola.

4 Marie-Galante, which is 61 square miles (158 square kilometres) in area.

5 The Dominican Republic (1844). The first, of course, was Haiti, forty years earlier.

6 Trinidad and Tobago, which became independent on 31 August 1962, less than a month after Jamaica.

7 Bequia is the largest of the Grenadines of St Vincent, but the largest of all the Grenadines is Carriacou, which belongs to Grenada and is a little more than twice the size of Bequia.

8 Bonaire is the second largest of the Netherlands Antilles in terms of area, but the much smaller St Maarten has a much bigger population. Curaçao is the largest in both area and population.

9 Vieques (57 square miles, 148 square kilometres) and Culebra (about 20 square miles, 52 square kilometres), both a few miles to the east of Puerto Rico itself.

10 The poet and playwright Derek Walcott, who won the Nobel Prize for Literature in 1992. The first was Sir Arthur Lewis, who won the Nobel Prize for Economics in 1979.

4 Just keeps rolling along

1. The Courantyne River forms the boundary between Guyana and Suriname.
2. Santo Domingo, capital of the Dominican Republic, stands on the Ozama River.
3. The River Artibonite is in Haiti and gives its name to the Département de l'Artibonite.
4. The American film star Errol Flynn.
5. Dunn's River Falls.
6. Dominica claims to have 365 rivers.
7. Barbados. The 'Indian Bridge' was the origin of the name Bridgetown.
8. The River Antoine Estate is home to a distillery which produces a fine overproof white rum called Rivers. The distillery grinds its own sugar cane using an ancient waterwheel powered with water from the river.
9. Going north along the Windward coast of St Vincent. It is normally possible to drive across the Rabacca Dry River, an expanse of volcanic rocks and boulders, but heavy rains can make it completely impassable.
10. What separates the two islands of Grande-Terre and Basse-Terre which make up Guadeloupe is called the Rivière Salée (Salt River), but it is a narrow arm of the sea and not a river at all.

5 Where are we?

1 The Pitons, St Lucia

2 El Morro, San Juan, Puerto Rico

3 The Columbus Lighthouse, Santo Domingo, Dominican Republic

4 Kaieteur Falls, Guyana

5 The Circus, Basseterre, St Kitts

6 Bridgetown, Barbados

7 Kingston, Jamaica

8 St John's, Antigua

9 Willemstad, Curaçao

10 Stollmeyer's Castle, Port of Spain, Trinidad

6 Not quite the same

1. Fallen Jerusalem is a small island near Virgin Gorda in the British Virgin Islands.
2. Sevilla La Nueva, named after the city of Seville (Sevilla) in Spain, was the original Spanish capital of Jamaica, begun in 1509 and abandoned in 1534 in favour of what became Spanish Town. Sevilla La Nueva was just west of the present town of St Ann's Bay, on the island's north coast, and some of its remains have been excavated.
3. New Amsterdam in Guyana, and Nieuw Amsterdam in Suriname.
4. Barbados.
5. Suriname, where there is a place called Totness (a common older spelling of the English name). Suriname was an English colony for a period in the 17th century.
6. Montserrat. Plymouth was abandoned as the capital after the volcanic eruptions of 1995 to 1997.
7. Tobago.
8. Nevis, the capital of which is Charlestown.
9. Basseterre is the capital of St Kitts, while Basse-Terre is the capital of Guadeloupe.
10. Georgetown is the capital of Guyana, while George Town is the capital of the Cayman Islands. There is also a Georgetown in St Vincent and another in the island of Great Exuma in The Bahamas.

7 ¡Que Bonita Bandera!

1	Haiti
2	Dominican Republic
3	Cuba
4	Puerto Rico
5	St Vincent and the Grenadines
6	Dominica
7	Guyana
8	Barbados
9	Montserrat
10	Aruba

8 I'll fly away...

1 Luis Muñoz Marín International Airport, San Juan, Puerto Rico.

2 José Martí, after whom the international airport in Havana, Cuba, is named. The song, of course, is 'Yo soy un hombre sincero', better known as *Guantánamera.*

3 The Queen Beatrix International Airport is in Aruba.

4 St Eustatius, where the airport is called after Franklin Delano Roosevelt (who did once see the island from the deck of a US naval vessel).

5 The Juancho E. Yrausquin Airport in Saba.

6 The official name of the airport for Santo Domingo in the Dominican Republic is the 'Aeropuerto Internacional Las Américas'.

7 St Lucia's Hewanorra International Airport is called after the Amerindian name for the island.

8 Paramaribo, Suriname, where the Zorg-en-Hoop Airport in a city suburb is used only for internal flights. International flights use the modern J. A. Pengel Airport outside the city.

9 Seawell. The Derek Walcott poem is *Tales of the Islands: Chapter X ('adieu foulard').*

10 The Centre Spatial Guyanais in Kourou, Guyane (French Guiana), is used for the European Space Agency's Ariane programme.

9 Sites and monuments

1 The stones at the pre-Columbian site at Capá are believed to mark a large ceremonial plaza, and a series of courts, one large and two smaller ones, used for a ball-game.

2 At La Isabela in Hispaniola, where Christopher Columbus founded a town in late 1493 or early 1494. The site is on the north coast of what is now the Dominican Republic, by the River Bajabonico. La Isabela lasted only a few years, replaced by Santo Domingo, founded on the south coast in 1498.

3 St. Kitts. 'The Gibraltar of the West Indies' was the fortress at Brimstone Hill, first used for military purposes in the 1690s, though most of the impressive fortifications still visible were built in the 1780s and 1790s.

4 At Betty's Hope in Antigua, which was one of the island's largest sugar plantations for some three centuries.

5 George Brydges Rodney, Lord Rodney (1718–1792). The Jamaican House of Assembly commissioned a monument to him after his victory over the French at the Battle of the Saints in 1782. A marble statue of the Admiral (dressed as a Roman emperor) was erected as the centrepiece of an imposing colonnade in Spanish Town, but it was moved to Kingston in 1872, before being returned to Spanish Town in 1889.

6 Horatio Nelson, Viscount Nelson (1758–1805), whose statue in Bridgetown, Barbados, was unveiled in 1813. The statue of him on top of the Nelson Column in London was not placed there until 1849.

7 The citadel of La Ferrière, on top of a mountain about 12 miles (19 kilometres) south of the town of Cap Haitien. An enormous fortress built between 1805 and 1820, its walls are up to 131 feet (40 metres) high and 13 feet (4 metres) thick.

8 Havana, Cuba. Made in 1631 and towering above the Castillo de la Real Fuerza, the 6 feet 6 inches (2 metres) high figure is known as La Giraldilla (The Weathercock) and is said to represent the wife of the 16th century governor Hernando de Soto. The brand of rum is, of course, Havana Club.

9 El Morro. There is another famous fortress of the same name in Havana, Cuba. The name means the headland, or promontory.

10 It was the home of Bob Marley, and is now a museum devoted to his life and music.

10 Disasters

1 Port Royal in Jamaica. Rebuilt after the earthquake, it continued as an important station for the British navy until the early 20th century.

2 The hurricane of 10–11 October 1780, which claimed thousands of lives throughout the eastern Caribbean, with Barbados and Martinique being particularly badly affected. This hurricane was perhaps the most costly ever recorded in terms of human life.

3 The cholera. It killed some 20 000 in Barbados alone in 1854.

4 Ciparis had been due to be hanged. He had received word of a reprieve the day before, but was still in the condemned cell on the fateful morning of 8 May 1902 – a fact which saved his life once more when the volcano of Montagne Pélée exploded. Ciparis was one of only two survivors out of some 30 000 people in the town of St-Pierre, because the condemned cell was solidly constructed and the single small window faced away from the volcanic blast.

5 Kingston, Jamaica. The damage was increased by a fire which broke out immediately after the earthquake.

6 The *Island Queen* was a schooner which left Grenada for St Vincent on 5 August 1944, with 67 people on board, and was never seen again. The disappearance has never been satisfactorily explained.

7 Jim Jones, a self-appointed 'messiah' from the USA, who persuaded more than 900 followers to join him in a mass suicide at their settlement at Jonestown in the Guyanese jungle.

8 Hurricane Gilbert caused severe damage in Jamaica in September 1988. Lovindeer's song enquired about the fate of his satellite dish.

9 Their islands were the ones worst hit by Hurricane Luis.

10 Montserrat, where the repeated eruptions of the Souffrière Hills Volcano forced the evacuation of the southern part of the island and led to the emigration of many of its inhabitants.

11 Animal geography

ANSWERS

1 The Dogs are north-east of Tortola in the British Virgin Islands.There is also a Dog Island near Anguilla.

2 Cat Island is in the Bahamas. It has nothing to do with the animal, but is named after a 17th century pirate called Arthur Catt.

3 St Lucia's Rat Island is the one which is home to a cultural foundation established by Derek Walcott, winner of the Nobel Prize for Literature.

4 The Cayman Islands, which were known as the Caymanas by 1530. The Spanish word caimán, meaning a New World crocodile, is of Amerindian origin.

5 The Dragon's Mouth is the channel at the northern end of the Gulf of Paria which separates Trinidad from Venezuela. The channel at the southern end of the Gulf of Paria is called the Serpent's Mouth.

6 The best known is an island off the north coast of Haiti, famous as a resort of the buccaneers in the 17th century, called Tortuga or Ile la Tortue (from the Spanish and French words for turtle). There is another Tortuga off the coast of Venezuela, and the tiny La Tortue off St Barthélemy (St Barts).

7 Grenada.

8 Both belong to Venezuela, but while the Aves Islands are a group about 100 miles (160 kilometres) off the Venezuelan mainland, there is also an Aves Island about 360 miles (579 kilometres) to the north-east, and 140 miles (225 kilometres) west of Dominica. It is small, low-lying and uninhabited.

9 Barbados. The harbour was constructed 1956–61.

10 In St Lucia. The island was Admiral Rodney's headquarters in 1782, just before the Battle of the Saints, and much of Fort Rodney can still be seen.

12 All manner of four-footed beasts

1 The manicou *(Didelphus marsupialis insularis).*

2 The tatou is a nine-banded armadillo *(Dasypus novemcinctus)* which you are most likely to see as one of the supporters of the national coat of arms of Grenada. Although still found in Trinidad, Grenada and St Vincent, the tatou has been hunted to the verge of extinction.

3 The red-legged tortoise or morocoy *(Geochelone carbonaria)*, once found virtually throughout the Caribbean, but now extinct in many islands.

4 A large frog *(Leptodactylus fallax)* found in Dominica and Montserrat. It is hunted for its hind legs, which are cooked and served to the ecologically insensitive as a delicacy.

5 The racoon *(Procyon minor)* is still found in Guadeloupe, though even there it is now very scarce. It used to be found in many other islands.

6 The Cockscomb Jaguar Reserve in south-central Belize is the only one of its kind in the world.

7 The Vervet or Green Monkey *(Cercopithecus aethiops sabaeus)* is found in Barbados and in St Kitts and Nevis, while the Mona Monkey *(Cercopithecus mona)* – a related species – is found in Grenada. Both species are believed to have been introduced into the Caribbean from Africa in the 17th century.

8 Barbados. A unique breed with hair rather than wool, the blackbelly sheep are often mistaken for goats by visitors. They are believed to have originated in Barbados as a cross between a European woolly variety and an African hair sheep.

9 The mongoose *(Herpestes javanicus).*

10 The camel – Richard Ligon describes camels being used as beasts of burden in his *True & Exact History of the Island of Barbados (1657).* While they could carry substantial loads, they were unsuited to the terrain and they do not appear to have continued in use for long.

13 Creeping and crawling things

1 Various species of lizard are called wood-slave in different parts of the Caribbean.

2 Found only in Barbados, St Lucia and Martinique, the world's smallest snake is the seldom seen *Leptotyphlops bilineata.*, sometimes called the 'seven years snake' or 'seven days snake' in Barbados. It grows to a little over three inches (9 centimetres) in length.

3 Some believe that if you steep a centipede in a bottle of rum, the resulting infusion makes a good general tonic and guarantees protection against centipede bites. Try it at your own risk!

4 A large ant which can give you a nasty bite if you fail to heed the warning it kindly gives of its approach – it makes an audible clicking sound with its jaws, hence the name.

5 The fer-de-lance (*Bothrops caribbaea*), a species of pit viper common in parts of South America and found in certain areas of St Lucia. Its bite can be fatal.

6 A species of stick insect (*Bostra maxwelli*), known as the god-horse in some parts of the Caribbean. It grows to about 13 inches (33 centimetres) in length.

7 Mabouya was originally an Amerindian word meaning a kind of evil spirit. The pale and ghost-like colour of some of the species of lizard now called mabouya perhaps earned them the name, though they are all harmless.

8 Iguanas are large lizards of several species which have been hunted and eaten by man in the Caribbean since pre-Columbian times; as a result the iguana is now extinct in some countries where it once flourished.

9 An insect (*Tunga penetrans*) which sometimes lays its eggs under the skin of humans. When these hatch, the creeping about of the larvae causes an intolerable itching, only relieved by digging out the offending creatures with a needle. Also called chigoe or jigger.

10 This used to be said of the railway which ran (if this is the word) in Barbados from 1881 to 1937. See Leviticus, xi, 41.

14 Feathered friends

1. The world's largest nesting colony of the Magnificent Frigate Bird (*Fregata magnificens*) is to be found in The Lagoon, Barbuda.

2. Patu is the name given in Jamaica to two local species of owl and a species of nightjar which is often mistaken for an owl. The word is West African in origin, a borrowing from Twi.

3. A colony of Birds of Paradise (originally from New Guinea) was introduced to a small island off Tobago in the early years of the 20th century, and the birds are also shown on the Trinidad and Tobago 100-dollar note. The 'Bird of Paradise' is also the common name for a species of flowering plant (*Strelitzia reginae*).

4. The coat of arms of the University of the West Indies has as its crest a Brown Pelican (*Pelicanus occidentalis*). This feeds by making spectacular dives into the sea to catch fish.

5. Bonaire, in the Netherlands Antilles, where the name of Flamingo Airport pays tribute to the pink flamingos (*Phoenicopterus ruber ruber*), which have chosen the island as one of their few nesting places.

6. Dominica (the Sisserou Parrot, *Amazonia imperialis*), St Lucia (the St Lucia Parrot, *Amazonia versicolor*), and St Vincent (the St Vincent Parrot, *Amazonia guildingii*). All three are found only in their respective islands; the first two are used as supporters of their respective countries' coats of arms.

7. The Cattle Egret (*Bubulcus ibis*), now found in more than fifty Caribbean islands.

8. The blackbird or Carib grackle (*Quiscalus lugubris*) is supposed to call 'Bequia sweet, sweet, sweet!', though entirely different versions of the blackbird's call are given in other islands.

9. The Scarlet Ibis (*Eudocimus ruber*).

10. The world's smallest hummingbird is the Bee Hummingbird (*Mellisuga helenae*), which is about 2 inches (5 centmetres) long, and is found only in Cuba.

15 Creatures of the sea and river

1 The cascadura (*Callicthys littoralis*).

2 Barbados.

3 Not a fish at all, but a pilot whale (*Globicephala macrorhyncus*), a marine mammal sometimes hunted in St Vincent and the Grenadines for its meat.

4 A large and edible fish (*Coryphaena hippurus*). Tourist restaurants sometimes describe it as 'not Flipper' to distinguish it from the marine mammal famous for its friendliness and ability to learn tricks in an aquarium. Alternatively, they use the Hawaiian name mahi-mahi (which will leave many local people baffled).

5 Although their numbers have been severely reduced worldwide by hunting, the humpback whale (*Megaptera novaeangliae*), which can weigh as much as 61 tons (60 tonnes), is still occasionally seen in parts of the Caribbean.

6 An octopus.

7 Still found in parts of the Caribbean – just – the Kemps Ridley turtle (*Lepidochelys kempi*) is the rarest of marine turtles, on the verge of extinction. It is also the smallest.

8 The mermaid legend is thought to be based on the manatee or sea-cow, a large marine mammal with two front flippers and a tail. The Antillean manatee (*Trichechus manatus*) is found in Florida and in isolated swampy areas of the larger Caribbean islands.

9 A species of crocodile (*Crocodylus acutus*) appears as the crest of the Jamaican coat of arms. Once common in the Black River and the swamps of the island's south coast – indeed, in the 17th century they swarmed in Kingston Harbour – the Jamaican crocodile is now very scarce. It is locally known as an alligator although, strictly speaking, a crocodile and an alligator are not the same.

10 Unlikely. The Caribbean Monk Seal (*Monachus tropicalis*), the only member of the seal family found in warm waters, was extremely common when Europeans arrived in the Americas at the end of the 15th century. Hunting for their oil and hides reduced them to the point of extinction by the end of the 19th century, and the last known sighting was in 1952. Folds of flesh on the creature's neck supposedly resembled those of a monk's cowl, hence the name.

16 Fruits of the earth

1 Now popular in many parts of the world, the grapefruit (*Citrus paradisi)* is thought to have originated in Barbados as a natural cross between the sweet orange (*C. sinensis*) and the shaddock (*C. grandis*), both of which were introduced from Asia.

2 The breadfruit was brought from Tahiti to the Caribbean in 1792 by Captain William Bligh of the Royal Navy, who made the voyage specially for the purpose. This was his second attempt – his first, in 1789, ended in the famous mutiny on the *Bounty*. The British government sought to introduce the breadfruit into the region as a nourishing item of diet for the slaves, who at first refused to eat it, but it became a popular food in many parts of the region.

3 The Blue Mountains of Jamaica offer ideal conditions for growing coffee. Its discovery by the Japanese has ensured that in recent years Blue Mountain coffee is the most expensive in the world. For many connoisseurs, the high price is simply a deserved tribute to its superlative quality.

4 Grenada, which is (with Indonesia) one of the world's two leading producers of nutmeg. The spice was introduced into Grenada from the East Indies in the 19th century.

5 The Antigua Black is a particularly sweet variety of pineapple for which the island is famous.

6 'Jamaica pepper' was an old name for allspice or pimento, which is still extensively cultivated in Jamaica.

7 This depends on your point of view. In Jamaica, ackee is a fruit (*Blighia sapida*) which is cooked and eaten as a vegetable. In Barbados, on the other hand, an ackee is an entirely different fruit (*Melicoccus bijugatus*), referred to in much of the Caribbean as a guinep or chenipe.

8 Cocoa. It declined sharply in importance in the 1920s, as a result of competition from other sources and the incidence of witchbroom disease.

9 Buxton Spice is a variety of mango, named after a village in Guyana.

10 Besides the Caricom countries of Dominica, St Lucia, St Vincent and the Grenadines, and Grenada, the French Overseas Departments of Martinique and Guadeloupe are also significant producers of bananas.

17 Pleasures of the table

1 Jamaica.

2 Boston Bay is regarded as the original home of jerked pork, a highly spiced delicacy now widely popular throughout Jamaica and beyond its shores.

3 Cassareep, a liquid made from cassava. It is a natural tenderiser.

4 Many people believe that the pudding will burst if you talk while it is being cooked.

5 Roti – a helping of curry (meat, vegetable, or occasionally shrimp) wrapped up in a pancake-like bread called a roti skin.

6 A soup made from the head and other less mentionable parts of a goat when the rest of the animal has been turned into curry. The name is derived from its alleged aphrodisiac qualities.

7 The conkie – a mixture of cornmeal, grated pumpkin and grated coconut, wrapped in a quailed (singed) banana leaf and steamed. Bajans eat conkies around Independence time (30 November), but before Independence in 1966, conkies had long been associated with Guy Fawkes' Day (5 November).

8 Fungi (the usual spelling, but pronounced 'fungee'). It is perhaps best described as a stiffish cornmeal porridge. Besides the cornmeal, the other ingredients vary from place to place; a Barbadian regards okras as essential, but in Grenada coucou is made with coconut milk. The name funchi (similar to the Antiguan pronunciation) is used further west, in Aruba, Bonaire and Curaçao.

9 Callaloo (a spinach-like vegetable) and pieces of crab-meat.

10 Arrowroot flour.

18 I'll drink to that!

1 Rum.

2 Barbados was the first Caribbean island to develop the manufacture of rum.

3 *Rhum agricole* is distilled from cane juice, while *rhum industriel* is distilled from molasses.

4 *Clairin* is a type of cheap white rum popular in Haiti.

5 This well-known rhyme gives the recipe for a traditional West Indian rum punch. The ingredients are: lime juice, sugar, rum and water (or ice).

6 Curaçao, where a local firm still makes the original Curaçao liqueur, which is flavoured with the peel of the laraha, a local bitter orange.

7 Aruba. The drink is called coecoei.

8 Only up to a point. The 'dry belly-ache' was actually lead poisoning, caused by the fact that some rum was then distilled in equipment with lead pipes.

9 Sangaree was once a popular drink in the Caribbean, particularly amongst the planter and merchant classes. The main ingredients were wine (often Madeira), lime juice, water, and spices such as nutmeg or cinnamon. The name probably has the same origin (i.e. meaning 'bloody') as the modern sangria, a rather different Spanish drink which tourism has made popular in other European countries. This is often just red wine and orange juice, with pieces of fruit floating in it.

10 Tia Maria, the popular coffee liqueur from Jamaica.

19 The sporting life

1. A hard one to answer, but it's almost certainly not cricket. Baseball is a strong contender: it is immensely popular in Cuba, the Dominican Republic and Puerto Rico, whose combined population is several times that of the English-speaking Caribbean. The Cubans have more than once beaten the USA at baseball in Olympic competition, and the Dominican Republic is an important source of professional baseball players for major US teams. In the Caribbean as a whole, soccer is also almost certainly well ahead of cricket in popularity.
2. The Cuban player, José Raúl Capablanca.
3. The Barbadian, Ronald 'Suki' King, who won the world three-move-restriction draughts championship in late 1994, adding it to the world go-as-you-please championship he already held.
4. Arthur Wint, of Jamaica, who won the 400 metres at the 1948 Olympics in London.
5. Teófilo Stevenson, of Cuba, who won the heavyweight gold medal at the 1972, 1976 and 1980 Olympic Games.
6. Anthony Nesty of Suriname.
7. Marie-José Perec.
8. Javier Sotomayor of Cuba, who cleared 7 feet 8 inches (2.2 metres)at the Barcelona Olympics, and 8 feet and 1/2 inch (2.4 metres) in Salamanca the following year.
9. Merlene Ottey of Jamaica, who had for years been placed among the medallists, but Stuttgart was her first gold at a major international meet.
10. Horse racing ceased to be held at the Queen's Park Savannah in Port of Spain, and moved to a new track at Arima.

20 Cricket, lovely cricket

1 *The Pickwick Papers*, by Charles Dickens. The very implausible description of a single-wicket match is given by the character Alfred Jingle, not noted for his veracity. The story is presumably the origin of the name of one of the leading cricket clubs in Barbados – Pickwick, founded in 1882.

2 The first 'inter-colonial match,' as such things used to be called, took place in 1846. British Guiana (now Guyana) and Barbados played each other twice, with each side winning a game.

3 An English side first toured the West Indies in 1895.

4 For a match in Trinidad in 1897. The West Indies won by three wickets.

5 In 1900.

6 In 1928, with the first Test Matches involving the West Indies taking place on their tour of England that year. England won all three matches.

7 The Third Test of the 1929-30 series against England, played at Bourda in 1930. The West Indies won by 289 runs, with the bowling of Learie Constantine playing a major part in the victory.

8 Sonny Ramadhin and Alf Valentine, who bowled the West Indies to victory in the 1950 series against England, taking 59 out of 77 English wickets between them.

9 Frank Worrell, Clyde Walcott and Everton Weekes – all eventually knighted in recognition of their outstanding contribution to the game.

10 Thirty-six years. Sobers made 365 not out in the Third Test against Pakistan at Sabina Park in 1958, a record which stood until Brian Lara's 375 not out against England at the Antigua Recreation Ground in April 1994.

21 Famous faces

1	Trinidadian calypsonian Denyse Plummer.
2	Trinidadian writer and philosopher, the late C. L. R. James, best known for *Beyond a Boundary*.
3	Trinidadian cricketer and world record holder, Brian Lara.
4	World-renowned reggae star, the late Bob Marley.
5	Guadeloupean novelist Maryse Condé.
6	Cuban leader Fidel Castro.
7	Dominican novelist Jean Rhys.
8	Cheddi Jagan, the late President of Guyana.
9	Dame Eugenia Charles, former Prime Minister of Dominica.
10	Michael Manley, late Prime Minister of Jamaica.

22 Go girl!

1 Anacaona.

2 Nanny of the Maroons.

3 Nanny Grig.

4 Sarah Ann Gill.

5 The Jamaican artist Edna Manley. Her sculpture and paintings transformed the arts of the English-speaking Caribbean in the 1930s and 1940s, showing new possibilities in indigenous culture. She also happened to be the wife of one major political leader (Norman Manley) and the mother of another (Michael Manley).

6 Beryl McBurnie. She took the Little Carib Dancers on several overseas tours, and choreographed the First World Festival of Negro Arts in Senegal in 1967.

7 Louise Bennett (the Hon. Louise Bennett Coverley).

8 Dame Hilda Bynoe, appointed Governor of Grenada in 1968.

9 Dame Mary Eugenia Charles, Prime Minister of Dominica 1980–1995.

10 Dame Nita Barrow of Barbados.

23 Let us now praise famous men

ANSWERS

1 Hatuey refused to be baptised, saying he had no desire to go to heaven if it was a place where he would be likely to meet any more Christians.

2 Chatoyer, now a National Hero of St Vincent and the Grenadines.

3 Julien Fédon, who hoped to make Grenada part of the new French Republic and abolish slavery. After the defeat of the rebels, Fédon disappeared and was never seen again.

4 Pierre Dominique Toussaint L'Ouverture, architect of the Haitian independence he never lived to see. Repeatedly victorious in battle, he was captured by treachery and died in a French prison in 1803.

5 Bussa, the ranger or head driver on Bayley's plantation in the parish of St Philip. He is believed to have been killed during the fighting.

6 Samuel Sharpe, now one of Jamaica's national heroes. He was hanged after the suppression of the rebellion.

7 Juan Pablo Duarte, Francisco del Rosario Sánchez and Ramón Mella were leaders of the struggle for the independence of the Dominican Republic from Haitian control in the 1840s.

8 Paul Bogle, a small farmer and Baptist deacon. The Morant Bay Rebellion was a major popular uprising against the injustices which prevailed in post-Emancipation Jamaican society, and led to significant changes in the government and administration of the colony. However, the uprising was suppressed with extreme brutality and Bogle was among those hanged. He is now one of Jamaica's national heroes.

9 Máximo Gómez y Páez, whose services to the Cuban nation are commemorated by a grandiose monument on the Havana waterfront.

10 Marcus Mosiah Garvey (1887–1940), now a national hero of Jamaica.

24 Servants of the people

1 The Barbadian politician, Sir Grantley Adams, was the first and only Prime Minister of the short-lived Federation of the West Indies (1958–1962).

2 Dr. Eric Williams, Premier (and later Prime Minister) of Trinidad and Tobago, who made this comment when Jamaica left the Federation of the West Indies after a referendum in that country in September 1961. Dr Williams was unwilling that Trinidad and Tobago should be left, as he saw it, with the burden of supporting the other, smaller and poorer, territories of the Federation. Trinidad and Tobago accordingly withdrew in January 1962, and the Federation soon collapsed, being formally dissolved at midnight on 31 May 1962.

3 Sir Eric Gairy, former Prime Minister of Grenada.

4 J.M.G.M. 'Tom' Adams, Prime Minister of Barbados 1976–1985, was the son of Sir Grantley Adams, who was Premier of Barbados 1954–1958, before he became Prime Minister of the Federation. The father of Michael Manley, Prime Minister of Jamaica 1972–1980 and 1989–1992, was Norman Manley, who was Chief Minister and later Premier of Jamaica, 1955–1962. Lester Bird became Prime Minister of Antigua and Barbuda in 1994, succeeding his father, Vere Bird, Senior, who headed the government of Antigua and Barbuda as Chief Minister, Premier and later Prime Minister, 1961–1971 and 1976–1994.

5 At the time of writing (2002), three Commonwealth Caribbean countries have presidents as their Heads of State: the Republic of Guyana, the Republic of Trinidad and Tobago, and the Commonwealth of Dominica.

6 Edward Seaga, Prime Minister of Jamaica 1980–1989.

7 None of the three was born in the country of which he later became prime minister. Edward Seaga and Lester Bird were both born in the United States of America, while John Compton was born in Canouan, in the Grenadines of St Vincent.

8 Erskine Sandiford, Prime Minister of Barbados, lost a parliamentary vote of confidence in 1994. He called general elections for later the same year, in which his party, under a different leader, was defeated.

9 Maurice Bishop, who became Prime Minister of Grenada in 1979 after his New Jewel Movement seized power from the government of Sir Eric Gairy in a bloodless coup, was deposed and murdered in 1983 by rivals within his own government. Democracy was restored soon afterwards by the intervention of troops and police from the United States and several neighbouring Caribbean countries.

10 President Jean-Bertrand Aristide, elected 1990, driven into exile in 1991, and restored to power in 1994.

25 A dangerous sort of people called pirates

1 A privateer had an official commission (often known as a Letter of Marque) from his country's government, which licensed him to attack enemy shipping in time of war. A pirate operated on his own account and was prepared to attack whatever ships he thought he could capture (including those of his own country) whether there was a war on or not.

2 *De Americaensche Zeerovers* (Amsterdam, 1678) by Alexander Olivier Exquemelin. The first English version appeared in London in 1684 as *The Buccaneers of America*, with the author's name given as John Esquemeling.

3 François L'Ollonais, a Frenchman who was killed by Indians in the Gulf of Darien not long afterwards.

4 Sir Henry Morgan (1635–1688).

5 Anne Bonny and Mary Read. They appear to have been active and willing pirates, but in the end they escaped the gallows (unlike Rackham) as a result of being pregnant.

6 Major Stede Bonnet (1688–1718), known as 'the Gentleman Pirate'.

7 Blackbeard was Captain Edward Teach (according to the most usual version of his name). His origins are obscure, though he is said to have been born in Jamaica. After some time as a privateer, he turned pirate in 1716 and preyed on shipping in the Caribbean and off the coast of North America for two years, before being killed in battle with a Royal Navy sloop at Oracroke Inlet, North Carolina, in 1718.

8 On a hill above Charlotte Amalie in St Thomas, in the United States Virgin Islands. The 'castle' is a fortified watch-tower built by the Danish colonial authorities in the 1680s. Now part of a hotel, it is a historical monument of some importance, but the connection with Blackbeard the pirate is unproven.

9 Barbados, where Sam Lord's Castle is an important tourist attraction. It is an elegant Georgian mansion, rather than a castle, and while the original Samuel Hall Lord (1778–1844) was a planter with few scruples when it came to money matters, there is no evidence that he was in any way responsible for the wrecks or that he deserved the reputation of a pirate which has been fastened on him by local legend and tourist brochures.

10 The Bahamas. The Latin motto (*Expulsis piratis, commercia restituta*) dated from 1728 and referred to the successful anti-pirate campaigns of Governor Woodes Rogers. Since 1971, the Commonwealth of the Bahamas has used a revised coat of arms with a different motto.

26 Want the doctor help with that?

1 The Federation of St Kitts and Nevis. Dr Denzil Douglas defeated Dr Kennedy Simmonds at the polls.

2 Guyana. Dr Cheddi Jagan, a dentist by profession, had been the first Premier of what was then still British Guiana from 1961 to 1964. Earlier he had been the effective leader of the government for two periods in the 1950s – the first of which ended when the British government suspended the colony's constitution in response to what it saw as the excessive radicalism of Dr Jagan's People's Progressive Party.

3 'Papa Doc' was François Duvalier, a medical doctor who became President of Haiti in 1957 and soon consolidated his rule by tyrannical methods, making himself President for Life. His son Jean-Claude 'Baby Doc' Duvalier (not a medical man) succeeded him on his death in 1971, but was forced into exile by a popular uprising in 1986.

4 Dr Eric Williams, first Prime Minister of Trinidad and Tobago. The most famous of his many books remains *Capitalism and Slavery* (1944), a revised version of the thesis which earned him the D. Phil. degree from the University of Oxford.

5 A large hummingbird (*Trochilus polytmus*), popularly known as the Doctor Bird. It is found only in Jamaica (though the name Doctor Bird is used in other islands for different species).

6 'The Doctor' is a traditional name (used at least since the early 18th century) for a breeze blowing inland from the sea and allegedly a bringer of health.

7 Strictly speaking, a bush-doctor is a practitioner of traditional medicine, who uses plants ('bush') for their curative properties, but the term sometimes refers to an obeah-man or sorcerer. The two professions were often exercised by the same individual (and occasionally still are).

8 A 'doctor-shop'.

9 Montego Bay, Jamaica, where Doctor's Cove Beach has been helping to attract visitors since before the First World War.

10 'I, John Lettsom.' This bit of doggerel sums up much of 18th century medical practice, but John Coakley Lettsom (1744-1815) was the most distinguished London physician of his day. Born on Little Jost van Dyke in the British Virgin Islands, he was a Quaker who freed all the slaves he owned in 1768. As a young man, he practised medicine for a brief period in Tortola.

27 Money makes the world go round

1. Start counting: there's the Bahamas dollar, the Barbados dollar, the Belize dollar, the Cayman Islands dollar, the Eastern Caribbean dollar, the Guyana dollar, the Jamaican dollar, the Trinidad and Tobago dollar, and the United States dollar. There is a Bermuda dollar as well. The official currency of Haiti is the gourde, but five gourdes are sometimes referred to as a Haitian dollar.

2. The British Virgin Islands and the Turks and Caicos Islands use the US dollar as their official currency.

3. The Cayman Islands dollar, which is fixed at CI$0.83 to US$1.00.

4. Seven – the EC dollar is used in Anguilla, Antigua and Barbuda, Grenada, Montserrat, St Lucia, St Kitts and Nevis, and St Vincent and the Grenadines.

5. Cuba and the Dominican Republic each have their own peso. You could also include the Columbian peso and the Mexican peso, which are the official currency in some Western Caribbean islands belonging to those countries.

6. In the French Overseas Departments of Martinique, Guadeloupe, and Guyane (French Guiana), which are politically part of France and use the Euro as their official currency.

7. The Dutch unit of currency was generally referred to in English as the guilder or florin. It has given its name to the Aruban florin, the Netherlands Antilles guilder and the Suriname guilder, which are all separate currencies.

8. Costa Rica and El Salvador have different currencies, but both are called the colón, after Christopher Columbus (in Spanish, Cristóbal Colón). Panama has the balboa, called after Vasco Nuñez de Balboa, the first European to set eyes on the Pacific Ocean. The Venezuelan bolívar is called after Simón Bolívar, the liberator of South America from Spanish rule.

9. Sugar, tobacco and cotton were all commonly used as money in the 17th century English Caribbean.

10. The 'piece of eight' was a silver coin struck in Spain or (more commonly) one of the Spanish American colonies, and originally worth eight reales. About the same size as the later United States silver dollar, the piece of eight was for centuries one of the commonest coins in the Caribbean, circulating in the colonies of other European powers as well as those of Spain itself.

28 First peoples

1 They are all words which (like a number of others, such as 'barbecue') have passed into English and other European languages from the Arawakan languages of the original Amerindian inhabitants of the Caribbean islands.

2 Cassava (*Manihot utilissima*).

3 Guanín was an alloy of gold and copper – apparently naturally occurring – used by the Amerindians of the Greater Antilles for ornaments and badges of rank.

4 Bohío was an Amerindian word used in the Greater Antilles for a type of house constructed on a framework of poles with a thatched roof and sides. The word is still current in the Spanish-speaking Caribbean with the meaning of a hut or shack.

5 A suitable tree would be cut down, shaped and hollowed out with a combination of hand-tools (originally of stone) and fire. The hollowed out tree could be stretched to widen it by using hot stones and pieces of wood wedged in the opening, and the sides could be built up with planking if necessary. Quite large boats could be constructed by this method, which is still used in parts of the Caribbean and by some indigenous peoples in South America.

6 In the eastern Caribbean as well as in the Greater Antilles, the Amerindian word zemi referred to both spirits and artistic representations of them, in stone, pottery or some more perishable material

7 Smoking tobacco. Although tobacco was widely cultivated in the Americas by indigenous peoples, Europeans first saw it when some was brought to Columbus in the Bahamas on his first voyage.

8 Apart from the fact that the conch itself could be used for food, the shell provided material for both ornaments and tools, especially in islands – such as Barbados – where hard stone was non-existent or hard to come by.

9 Cacique. Originally referring to the ruler of a substantial area and number of people in the Greater Antilles, the word is still used in Spanish (particularly in South America) to mean a political strongman or party boss, often with the suggestion of despotism.

10 In small numbers only, in Dominica and St Vincent. The Garifuna of Belize are descendants of Black Caribs (people of mixed Amerindian and African descent) exiled from St Vincent by the British after the Carib War of 1795-96. The populations of the Hispanic Caribbean and Aruba are of partly Amerindian descent, but the original inhabitants of unmixed Amerindian origin had almost entirely vanished from the Greater Antilles within half a century of the arrival of Columbus, from a combination of exposure to European diseases, forced labour and deliberate massacre.

29 Principalities and powers

1. Gustavia, the capital of the island of St Barthélemy (St Barts), is called after Gustavus III, King of Sweden from 1771 to 1792. Now part of the French Department of Guadeloupe, the island was a Swedish colony (the only one in Caribbean history) from 1784 to 1877.

2. Tumble Down Dick Bay is said to be named for Richard Cromwell, Lord Protector of England, Scotland and Ireland from September 1658 to May 1659.

3. Prince William Henry, later King William IV (reigned 1830 to 1837).

4. Jean-Jacques Dessalines, Emperor of Haiti as Jacques Ier from 1804 until his assassination in 1806.

5. Henri Christophe, ruler of northern Haiti from 1807, and King Henri from 1811 until his suicide in 1820.

6. Faustin Soulouque, who became President of Haiti in 1847, and then ruled as the Emperor Faustin Ier from 1849 until his overthrow in 1859.

7. The Church (later Cathedral) of St John the Baptist, Belize City. The Kings of the Mosquitoes, or Miskito Indians, were George Frederick (crowned 1816), Robert Charles (1825), and George Augustus Frederick (1845). Their people's territory was claimed by Great Britain as a protectorate from 1655 to 1850. Still known as the Mosquito Coast, it now forms part of the Republic of Nicaragua.

8. In the churchyard of St John's, Barbados, is the tomb of Ferdinando Paleologus (died 1670), who claimed descent from Thomas the brother of Constantine XI Paleologus, the last of the Byzantine Emperors, who was killed in battle when Constantinople (Istanbul) fell to the Turks in 1453.

9. Martinique. Apart from the well-known Marie Rose Josephine Tascher de la Pagerie (1763–1814), who as the wife of Napoleon was Empress of the French, 1804–1809, Martinique was also the birthplace of Aimée Dubuc de la Rivery (c.1775–1817), who is said to have become the favourite wife of Selim III, Sultan of Turkey.

10. Angostura Aromatic Bitters. The product won a medal at the international exhibition in Vienna in 1873, and the medal, on which the Emperor Franz Josef's portrait appears, is reproduced on the label to this day.

30 Curiosities of colonialism

1 Dominica. The island was originally included by the British among the Windwards in 1763, but became a separate colony in 1771. From 1833 until 1940 Dominica was included in the Leeward Islands, which formed a single government under the colonial power. In 1940, it was placed with the Windwards once more, a grouping which has survived the independence of the various islands concerned, in geography if not in politics.

2 St Thomas, St Croix and St John, together with a number of much smaller islands dependent on them, were a Danish colony until 1917, when they were bought by the United States of America for US$25 million. They have since been known as the United States Virgin Islands.

3 The island of Hispaniola is shared by Haiti and the Dominican Republic. Part of St Martin belongs to the French Department of Guadeloupe, while the other part (known as Sint Maarten) belongs to the Netherlands Antilles.

4 Anguilla, the British Virgin Islands, the Cayman Islands, Montserrat, and the Turks and Caicos Islands. Bermuda may be added to the list, but is strictly speaking in the North Atlantic, not the Caribbean.

5 Haiti, which occupied the former Spanish territory which is now the Dominican Republic from 1822 to 1844.

6 After being independent from 1844, the Dominican Republic returned to Spanish rule in 1861. However, dissatisfaction soon set in, and armed revolt led to the restoration of independence in 1865.

7 Tobago. In the 17th century, successive Dukes of Courland (a Baltic principality which is now part of Latvia) sent several colonising expeditions to the island.

8 St Barthélemy (St Barts) was a Swedish colony (the only one in Caribbean history) from 1784 to 1877. It is now part of the French Department of Guadeloupe.

9 Cuba and Puerto Rico, which Spain lost as a result of the Spanish-American War of 1898.

10 St Eustatius, which was ruled at different times by the British, the French and the Dutch. When the island became Dutch for the final time in 1816, this was its twenty-third change of flag in less than two centuries.

31 Africa and the Caribbean

1 It was once a major centre of the transatlantic slave trade, and the point from which many thousands of Africans were forcibly transported to the Americas.

2 Some 350 years, from the early 16th century on. Most of the countries involved officially abolished the slave trade in the early 19th century, though slaves were still being brought into Cuba illegally until the early 1860s. There is still disagreement among historians as to the total number of victims.

3 Olaudah Equiano (c. 1745–1797), also known by the European name he later adopted, Gustavus Vassa. His *Life* was first published in 1789.

4 Edward Wilmot Blyden (1832–1912).

5 Kamau Brathwaite.

6 'You' (in the plural) – derived from the Igbo *unu*, with the same meaning. The word is also used in Belize and by speakers of Creole English in Nicaragua.

7 Warri, a game of the pit and pebble family which can be traced back more than 3000 years to Ancient Egypt. It is known in some other parts of the world as mancala.

8 A type of savings scheme of West African origin, still popular in some parts of the Caribbean. Members contribute equal amounts on a regular basis; each member has a turn to receive the total amount for the agreed period.

9 Milton King was a Barbadian seaman who died in South Africa in 1951 after a beating from a policeman – who later received a small fine. Milton King's death led to the first organised protests in the Caribbean against the apartheid regime in South Africa.

10 It is a tribute to the ideas of the Jamaican-born Pan-Africanist, Marcus Garvey, and the Black Star shipping line which he founded as a symbol and example of black economic independence.

32 Vive la France!

1 Martinique, Guadeloupe and Guyane (French Guiana).

2 Haiti, which from the later 17th century until the revolution of 1791 was the French colony of St-Domingue.

3 A group of small islands (in French, the Iles des Saintes) just south of Guadeloupe and within sight of Dominica. It was in the waters surrounding them that the British admiral Sir George Rodney defeated the French admiral the Comte de Grasse, on 12 April 1782. The battle saved Jamaica from capture by the French and introduced a new manoeuvre, that of 'breaking the line', into the naval tactics of the day.

4 Because they were for a century the site of a penal colony; one of them is the notorious Ile du Diable (Devil's Island). They lie off the coast of Guyane.

5 St Lucia, which was a French colony for several periods of its history before 1803.

6 St Kitts; the island was ceded wholly to the English by the Peace of Utrecht (1713).

7 Victor Schoelcher (1804–1893), commemorated in Martinique's Bibliothèque Schoelcher and many street and place names in the French Caribbean, played a major part in the abolition of slavery in the French colonies in 1848.

8 Félix Éboué (1884–1944).

9 Alexis Saint-Léger Léger (1887–1975), better known under his pen-name Saint-John Perse.

10 Aimé Césaire (born 1913). His most famous work, *Cahier d'un retour au pays natal* (*Return to my native land*), first published in 1939, was an inspiration to independence movements in French Africa.

33 Let's go Dutch

1. The capital of Aruba and the capital of St Eustatius are both called Oranjestad.

2. Both Oranjestad in Aruba and Kralendijk in Bonaire are sometimes called Playa, a Papiamentu word which simply means 'beach' and refers to the fact that the two towns are each sited on the main landing place in their respective islands.

3. The Kingdom of the Netherlands consists of the Netherlands themselves (i.e. the European country often referred to as Holland), the Netherlands Antilles, and Aruba.

4. Five – the Netherlands Antilles (a self-governing territory since 1954) consist of Curaçao, Bonaire, Sint Maarten (the Netherlands Antilles section of the island of St Martin), Sint Eustatius and Saba.

5. Aruba left the Netherlands Antilles on 1 January 1986.

6. Sint Eustatius is the official name of Statia.

7. By the Treaty of Breda (1667), the Dutch received Suriname in exchange for their North American settlement of Nieuw Amsterdam, better known by the name which the English then gave it – New York.

8. After the best part of three centuries as a Dutch colony and later (from 1954) a self-governing part of the Kingdom of the Netherlands, Suriname became independent in 1975.

9. The Dutch were the original European colonisers of Demerara, Essequibo and Berbice, which were captured by the British in 1803 and formally ceded to Britain in 1814-15. The three colonies were united to form British Guiana, which became independent as Guyana in 1966. The Dutch also occupied part of northern Brazil, 1630-1654.

10. Confusingly, Dutch usage is the opposite of the English on this point. For the Dutch, the Leeward Islands are Aruba, Curaçao and Bonaire, just north of the Venezuelan mainland. The Windward Islands are St Maarten, St Eustatius and Saba – which lie in the middle of what most English-speaking people in the Caribbean call the Leeward Islands.

34 The American connection

1 From Barbados. Tituba was a central figure in the notorious Salem witch trials of 1692.

2 Barbados, where George Washington (then aged 19) stayed for several weeks in 1751. He was accompanying his brother Lawrence, who was travelling for health reasons. Ironically, George caught the smallpox while in the island.

3 Alexander Hamilton, whose portrait appears on the US$10 bill, was born on 11 January 1757 in Charlestown, Nevis, where his birthplace can still be seen.

4 In St Eustatius in the Netherlands Antilles, where on 16 November 1776 the governor, Johannes de Graaff ordered a salute to be fired to the brig *Andrew Doria* of the Continental Navy, which was flying the Grand Union Flag. (The Stars and Stripes was not adopted until the following year.)

5 Port-au-Prince, Haiti, has an Avenue John Brown.

6 Spain lost her last remaining colonies in the Caribbean. Cuba became nominally independent, remaining however for many years effectively subordinated to the USA. Spain ceded Puerto Rico (and, on the other side of the world, the Philippines) to the United States.

7 At Guantánamo Bay, in Cuba. Since 1959, the Cuban government has refused to recognise the validity of the 1903 treaty by which Cuba leased the site to the United States, maintaining that the treaty was signed under coercion.

8 Since 1952, Puerto Rico has been a self-governing Commonwealth in association with the USA. The island has its own elected governor and congress. Puerto Ricans are US citizens, but they do not vote in federal elections.

9 In 1940, an agreement between the United States and Britain gave the USA 99-year leases on a number of naval bases in what were then British colonies in the Caribbean (Antigua, the Bahamas, Guyana, Jamaica, St Lucia and Trinidad) as well as in Newfoundland and Bermuda, in exchange for fifty over-age destroyers. As a result, large numbers of US naval personnel were stationed in these territories.

10 Navassa Island, which has been claimed by the United States since 1857. The United States Coastguard maintains an unmanned lighthouse on the island.

35 Asia and the Caribbean

ANSWERS

1. A few indentured labourers were brought from India to British Guiana in 1838, but the main period of this system was from 1845 to 1917.
2. A total of 238 909 indentured labourers were brought from India to British Guiana, and 143 939 to Trinidad.
3. The *Fatel Rozach* was the first ship to bring Indian immigrants to Trinidad, in 1845.
4. Most parts of the Caribbean have at least some Indian element in their population, but apart from Guyana and Trinidad, it is particularly significant in Suriname, Jamaica and Guadeloupe.
5. China (particularly to Cuba, Jamaica, Trinidad, Guyana, Suriname and Guyane [French Guiana]) and Java (to Suriname). Many Caribbean countries have small but significant populations of Arab descent, mainly from Syria and the Lebanon.
6. Hosay. It has lost much of its religious character, and has become more of a purely festive occasion, to the extent that it is disowned by some Muslims. Many non-Muslims and non-Indians take part.
7. Popular in Trinidad, chutney is a lively traditional form of Indian music, often accompanied by dancers.
8. The Hajj. Many Caribbean Muslims have made this pilgrimage.
9. Abeer is the coloured water which participants throw on each other as a sign of rejoicing during Phagwah, a Hindu spring festival.
10. Celebrated in the Caribbean, as in other parts of the world, Divali is a Festival of Lights in honour of Lakshmi, the Hindu goddess of good fortune.

36 The sweet negotiation of sugar

1 The sugar-cane is indigenous to the South Pacific.

2 As cultivated today, the sugar-cane is a complex hybrid of several different species of the genus *Saccharum*.

3 It was brought from the Canary Islands (where it had been cultivated by the Spanish for several years) to Hispaniola by Columbus on his second voyage in 1492.

4 The Sugar Revolution is the name given by modern historians to the process, which began in Barbados in the 1640s and 1650s and spread from there to other islands, whereby the production of sugar for export to European markets, using the labour of slaves imported from Africa, became the dominant economic activity.

5 Holes about 2–3 feet (0.6–0.9 metres) square and 5–6 inches (12–15 centimetres) deep dug in the fields; the planting of cane in these holes was intended to reduce soil erosion and provide for more economical use of fertiliser. The cane-hole system was popular in sugar-producing territories from the 18th to the 20th centuries, but it was very labour intensive and has been replaced in modern times by planting the cane in mechanically tilled furrows.

6 The first attempt to apply steam power to the crushing of canes was made by John Stewart in Jamaica in 1768, but the first successful use of steam for the purpose occurred in Cuba later in the 18th century, perhaps in 1797.

7 Making use of the fact that any liquid will boil at a lower temperature under reduced pressure, the vacuum-pan made more economical use of fuel and allowed the production of better quality sugars than the traditional method of boiling the juice in open tayches. The first vacuum-pan in the Caribbean was installed in Guyana in 1832.

8 Irenaeus Brathwaite Harper (c. 1821–1886) who saw them in 1858 when he was supervisor of a weeding gang at Highland Plantation in Barbados and recognised them for what they were. It was previously believed that all cane seed was sterile, and cane was propagated solely by the planting of cuttings. Harper's discovery ultimately made possible the development of new sugar cane varieties which have been of major importance to the industry in many parts of the world.

9 Achard (1753–1821) was the German chemist who made practicable the production of beet sugar – a discovery which, since the later 19th century, has ensured continuous and often ruinous competition for cane sugar.

10 Cuba.

37 Cultural miscellany

1 'Moko jumbie' is the name used in several parts of the English-speaking Caribbean for a performer on stilts – a frequent sight on festive occasions. The name 'stilt-man' or 'tilt-man' is used in other parts of the region.

2 Anansi.

3 An attempt by the authorities to ban Carnival. Canboulay (from Creole, *cann boulé* meaning 'Canes burning') was a synonym for Carnival.

4 *Jerningham the Governor* is usually regarded as the first Trinidad calypso to be sung entirely in English, rather than the French creole usual up to that date.

5 Barbados, whose now very popular Crop Over festival was started in 1974 as a revival of traditional celebrations associated with the end of Crop-time (the sugar-cane harvest).

6 The Roi Vaval, a symbolic figure who is the 'King of Carnival' – participants dress in black and white for his funeral, which brings the Carnival festivities to a close.

7 The Bahamas. Junkanoo is a traditional costumed festival, noticeably different in character from the Trinidad-style carnivals popular in many Caribbean islands.

8 The calypso was the classic *Rum and Coca-Cola*. The Trinidadian calypsonian Lord Invader (Rupert Grant) won the court case after proving he was the original composer, not the American comedian Morey Amsterdam, who had heard the song in Trinidad and went on to adapt and popularise it in the United States.

9 The original Wailers were Bob Marley (Robert Nesta Marley), Peter Tosh (Winston Hubert McIntosh) and Bunny Wailer (Neville O'Riley Livingstone), who sang together from 1963 to 1973.

10 The famous Trinidadian designer of Carnival bands, Peter Minshall.

38 Many mansions

1. According to early Spanish sources, Yocahu was the name of the supreme god, the giver of cassava, among the Amerindians of the Greater Antilles.
2. Antonio Montesinos (died 1545).
3. Bartolomé de las Casas (1484-1576).
4. The Unitas Fratrum (Unity of the Brethren), generally known as the Moravian Church, whose first missionaries to the Caribbean arrived in St Thomas, Danish West Indies (now USVI) in 1732.
5. Nathaniel Gilbert was the Speaker of the Antigua House of Assembly; he became a Methodist in 1758 while on a visit to England, and on his return to Antigua in 1760 he introduced Methodism to the Caribbean.
6. With a group of American Loyalists who came to Jamaica rather than accept the new United States of America and reject their allegiance to the British Crown. The first Baptist Church in Jamaica was established by the Reverend George Liele, an African American who came to Jamaica in 1783. The first white missionary from England did not arrive until 1814.
7. Not until 1824, when Christopher Lipscomb and William Hart Coleridge were consecrated as Bishops of Jamaica and of Barbados and the Leeward Islands, respectively. They arrived in the Caribbean at the beginning of the following year. Before this the Anglican Church in the Caribbean was generally regarded as falling under the jurisdiction of the Bishop of London.
8. Shango. In Trinidadian Shango, Shango himself is only one of several 'powers' who are invoked by followers of the cult.
9. Papa Legba, generally envisaged as a limping grandfather.
10. Members of the Rastafari faith accept the divinity of the late Emperor of Ethiopia, Haile Selassie I, whose title before his coronation was Ras Tafari (or Crown Prince, in the Amharic language of Ethiopia).

39 Godliness and good learning

1. Founded in 1538 by Pope Paul III, the University of St Thomas Aquinas in Santo Domingo was the first university in the Americas.

2. Codrington College in Barbados, whose history goes back to 1710, is the oldest theological college in the Anglican communion.

3. In 1690, Lady Mico, a rich English widow, left a sum of money to her nephew on condition that he marry one of her late husband's unmarried nieces, failing which, the money was to be used to ransom Christian slaves from the Barbary pirates in North Africa. The nephew did not marry as required, and after a while there were no more Christian slaves left to rescue from Barbary (modern Algeria). Left unused, the money accumulated for a considerable time, but in 1834 the British government decided to use it to establish a number of primary schools in the West Indies for educating the children of the newly emancipated slaves. One of these schools, which had a teacher-training department attached to it, became the present-day Mico College in Kingston, Jamaica, which is still a teacher-training college.

4. The Rawle Institute, for the training of primary school teachers, was attached to Codrington College, Barbados. It functioned from 1912 to 1945. It was named after Richard Rawle (1812-1889), a former principal of Codrington College and first Anglican bishop of Trinidad.

5. Captain J.O.Cutteridge compiled the *Nelson's West Indian Readers.*

6. Sparrow's calypso *Dan Is The Man In The Van* (1963) mocked the *Nelson's West Indian Readers.*

7. The University of the West Indies was established at Mona in Jamaica in 1948. Originally part of the University of London (as the University College of the West Indies), it became a fully independent institution in 1962.

8. The Imperial College of Tropical Agriculture, which had been established in 1921.

9. The Barbados campus of the University of the West Indies began on a temporary site at the Deep Water Harbour in 1963. It moved to its present location at Cave Hill in 1966.

10. The Caribbean Examinations Council was established in 1973.

40 I was glad...

1 Built between 1523 and 1540, the cathedral of Santa María de la Encarnación in Santo Domingo, Dominican Republic, is the oldest in the Americas.

2 The oldest Anglican cathedral outside the British Isles is that of St Jago de la Vega in Spanish Town, Jamaica. Built on the site of an older church, the present building was originally completed in 1714, although there are some later additions. Strictly speaking, the claim needs two modifications. St Thomas's Cathedral, Bombay, was begun much earlier (1672), though not completed until 1718. And if you include the Protestant Episcopal Church in the USA, they have a Spanish cathedral (that of San José de Gracia) in Mexico City which dates back to the 17th century.

3 St George's Cathedral, Georgetown, Guyana, is claimed to be the largest wooden church in the world.

4 The Synagogue Mikve Israel-Emanuel in Willemstad, Curaçao, which was completed and consecrated in 1732, is the oldest synagogue in continuous use in the Americas. The synagogue is the fourth in Curaçao, the first in the island having been consecrated in 1654. The original synagogue in Barbados dates back to the same period, but was destroyed in the 1831 hurricane, and the present synagogue dates from 1833. There is also a synagogue building in Nevis which has been claimed as the oldest in the Americas, but this has been a ruin for more than two centuries.

5 Paramaribo, Suriname.

6 Kingstown, St Vincent.

7 The (Protestant Episcopal) Cathedral of the Holy Trinity in Port-au-Prince, Haiti, completed 1928. In 1947, the then bishop, Alfred Voegeli, accepted a suggestion to have Haitian artists add pictures to what had been the severely plain interior of the church. This took place over several years, and together with the bishop's own collecting of Haitian paintings, did much to draw international attention to Haiti's indigenous art.

8 Dunstan St Omer, whose best known works include murals in the Cathedral in Castries, and in country churches at Roseau and Monchy in St Lucia.

9 Gustave Eiffel (1832-1923), famous for the landmark which bears his name in Paris, was also the designer of the cathedral in Fort-de-France, Martinique.

10 Christ Church, Barbados, where what is known as the Chase Vault is still shown to visitors, although it has long been empty. On five separate occasions in the early 19th century, the apparently securely sealed vault was opened and a number of lead coffins were found moved from the positions in which they had been left at the previous interment. No satisfactory explanation for the disturbances has ever been produced. In 1820, all the coffins were removed and buried in the churchyard.

41 Art and artists

1. Agostino Brunias. Some of his paintings were reproduced as engravings in Bryan Edwards' famous *History of the West Indies* (1794).
2. Dr William Thornton (1761–1828), a native of Tortola, where he practised medicine for two years before eventually settling in the USA. He had no formal training as an architect.
3. Michel Jean Cazabon (1813–1888). He exhibited in Paris in his youth, but returned to Trinidad in 1848, living and working there as a professional artist until his death.
4. Camille Pissarro (1830–1903).
5. Paul Gauguin (1848–1903).
6. Wilfredo Lam (1902–1982).
7. Kapo (otherwise Mallica Reynolds). Many of his works are on display in the National Gallery of Jamaica.
8. Aubrey Sendall Williams (1926–1990).
9. Karl Broodhagen.
10. Christopher Gonzalez, whose statue aroused considerable controversy because of its symbolic, rather than realistic treatment of its subject. The more conventional statue of Marley displayed outside the National Stadium in Kingston is by Alvin Marriott.

42 Also known as...

1 Alphonsus Cassell

2 Slinger Francisco

3 Aldwyn Roberts

4 Leroy Calliste

5 Rafael de Leon

6 Winston Peters

7 Austin Lyons

8 Garnet Smith

9 Anthony Carter

10 Stedson Wiltshire

43 Music, maestro!

1	Jamaica
2	Trinidad
3	Dominican Republic
4	Curaçao, Aruba and Bonaire
5	Martinique and Guadeloupe
6	Barbados
7	Jamaica
8	Dominican Republic
9	Cuba
10	Trinidad

44 Talk yuh Talk!

1 Spanish is the main language of the Caribbean. In second place comes Haitian Creole, the only language of most of Haiti's seven million or so inhabitants, which has more speakers than all forms of English in the Caribbean put together.

2 The mother tongue of most people in Aruba, Bonaire and Curaçao is Papiamentu, a creole based on Spanish and Portuguese, which also contains African, Dutch, English and even Hebrew elements. Dutch is the official language, and many people are also familiar with English and Spanish.

3 Sranan Tongo (literally, 'the Surinamese language') is an English-based creole with a history dating back to the 17th century. It is widely used in Suriname as a means of communication between speakers of the many different languages in use in the country.

4 Six: the official languages are French and Dutch, whilst the mother tongue of indigenous St-Martiners is a creole English. Immigrants from Haiti, the Dominican Republic, the rest of the Netherlands Antilles and Aruba add Haitian Creole, Spanish and Papiamentu.

5 Hindi and Urdu can be found in Trinidad, Guyana, and Suriname, while Suriname has significant numbers of Javanese speakers. Jewish communities keep Hebrew as a liturgical language. The region's Muslims use Arabic for religious purposes, while some members of the Syrian-Lebanese communities (who are mostly Christians) also retain a knowledge of Arabic. Some of the Chinese in the Caribbean, particularly in Cuba and Suriname, still know their ancestral language.

6 Haiti, and the French Overseas Departments of Martinique, Guadeloupe (and its out-islands, including St Bart's and the French part of St Martin) and Guyane (French Guiana).

7 As a result of the large number of Dutch plantation owners in St Thomas (then a Danish colony) in the 18th century, a Dutch-based creole developed and became the common language of the slaves there, and in the other Danish islands of St Croix and St John. Moravian missionaries turned it into a written language, and many slaves were literate in it. However, it lost ground to English in the 19th century and became extinct.

8 Trinidad. In the last years of the island's occupation by the Spanish (1783–1797), many French planters came to Trinidad from other parts of the Caribbean, bringing their slaves with them.

9 Dominica and St Lucia.

10 Puerto Rico has had both Spanish and English as official languages since 1902, with the exception of a brief period from 1991 to 1993, when Spanish was the sole official language.

45 More in the mortar...

1. Play wid puppy, puppy lick yuh mout'. (Another version has: Play wid puppy, puppy lick yuh mout'; play wid dog, dog bite yuh.)
2. Empty bag can't stand.
3. What sweet in goat mout' sour in 'e bam-bam.
4. Parson christen 'e own pickney first.
5. Stone a' river-bottom na know how de sun hot.
6. Every skin-teet' ain't a laugh.
7. Two man rat can't live in de same hole. (Sometimes heard with other animals, e.g. 'Two man crab...')
8. Duppy know who to frighten. (A well-known variant is 'High wind know where ol' house live'.)
9. Yuh can hide an' buy ground, but yuh can't hide an' work it.
10. De higher monkey climb, de more 'e show 'e tail.

and in case you're wondering about the title of this quiz, the complete proverb is *'There is more in the mortar than the pestle'.*

46 Songs my mother taught me

1 The original of *Yellow Bird* is a Haitian lullaby called *Choucounne*.

2 'Ah ain't kill nobody but me husband, so ah facin' de judge independent.' This folk-song is claimed by both Barbados and Trinidad, but Barbados perhaps has the better claim: one version gives names which can be identified with a real incident in Barbados in the 1870s.

3 As the Jamaican song (also known in other parts of the Caribbean) has it, 'Sammy plant piece a corn down a gully'.

4 She took her ackees to Linstead Market, but 'not a quatty wut [worth] sell'. In Jamaica, a quatty was a small silver coin, originally a quarter (hence the name) of a Spanish *real*, later a penny-halfpenny.

5 Usually, *There's a brown girl in the ring*, but other versions exist. One early one from Jamaica has 'a black boy'.

6 That's what her common-law husband said, according to a Barbadian folk-song from the 1920s. But in fact, the song explains, she was found 'down in de well' and 'Wid de wiah tie up she wais'/An' de razor cut up she face.'

7 In the song *Colón Man*, fun is made of the West Indian labourer who has been to Colón (to work on the Panama Canal), and returned home with more money than he had when he left – but not with more sense. He now wears a watch and chain – 'Wid him brass chain a lick him belly' – but he still can't tell the time.

8 Ja Ja was King of Opobo in what is now Nigeria. He fell out with the British, who exiled him to the Caribbean in 1891. He spent two and a half months in Barbados, where a still popular folk-song commemorates his alleged infatuation for a local woman called Becca, or, in other versions, Dovey.

9 Versions of *Sly Mongoose* are found all round the region, but in most of them the chicken ends up in his waistcoat pocket.

10 *Michael, row the boat ashore.*

47 The Fourth Estate

1 Jamaica. With a continuous history going back to 1834, the *Gleaner* is the oldest newspaper in the English-speaking Caribbean.

2 Barbados. Founded in 1895, the *Advocate* is the second oldest newspaper in the English-speaking Caribbean.

3 Cuba. *Granma* is named after the yacht which brought Fidel Castro and 82 revolutionaries to Cuba from their Mexican exile in December 1956, on their way to the eventual success of the revolution in January 1959.

4 *Listín Diario* is one of the leading papers in the Dominican Republic.

5 Published in Guyana, *Stabroek News* takes its title from an old name for Georgetown, also commemorated in the famous Stabroek Market.

6 *De Ware Tijd* is the main paper in Suriname. The Dutch title may be roughly translated as 'The real news'.

7 The *Labour Spokesman* is the organ of the St Kitts Labour Party.

8 Published in Antigua, *Outlet* was for many years the only real opposition media and it remains famous for its unique and combative style.

9 *France-Antilles* is published (in different editions) in Martinique and Guadeloupe.

10 The *Crusader* is one of several newspapers published in St Lucia.

48 Where did I read about them?

1. Annie Palmer, a legendary Jamaican character who made her fictional debut in H.G.de Lisser's *The White Witch of Rose Hall* (1929). She worked obeah to control her slaves, ruthlessly disposed of her husbands and anybody else who got in her way, and enjoyed innumerable lovers. Rose Hall is a real place, occupied by a real Annee May Palmer in the early 19th century, but how far her behaviour gave rise to the legend is questionable.

2. Ganesh Ramsumair, in V.S.Naipaul's 1957 novel, *The Mystic Masseur*, which recounts how Ganesh transforms himself from failed primary school teacher and ineffectual masseur into a healing mystic and politician, thereby raising himself from near the bottom of Trinidad's social heap to a seat on the Legislative and Executive Councils of the colony.

3. In Samuel Selvon's story, 'Brackley and the Bed', Brackley gets married to his cousin Teena, who has come from Tobago to join him in the middle of a London winter, because that is the only way she is going to let him sleep with her in the only bed in his room. But right after the wedding, Teena tells him that Aunty is arriving from Tobago the same evening. Of course, it will be Aunty, not Brackley, who will be sharing the bed with Teena.

4. It is Beccka who asks the question 'Do angels wear brassieres?' in Olive Senior's story of that name (published in *Summer Lightning*, 1986). This embarrasses a visiting Archdeacon and creates total chaos at home, but she eventually gets an answer from her friend Mr O'Connor: 'Well Beccka, as far as I know only the lady angels need to'.

5. King Henri Christophe of Haiti is the subject of both Walcott's *Henri Christophe* (1950) and Césaire's *La Tragédie du Roi Christophe* (1963).

6. Mittelholzer's *Kaywana* trilogy (1952–54) tells the story of the van Groenwegel family.

7. Tantie Merle, who causes such confusion in Paul Keens-Douglas's famous *Tantie at de Oval.*

8. Alan Holmes, in Ian McDonald's novel, *The Humming-Bird Tree.* Alan is a young white Creole Trinidadian boy, while Kaiser and Jaillin are East Indian children who work for his family. Alan realises that they are friends he must 'keep in a separate compartment' of his life: inevitably, the colonial society's attitudes to race and class destroy the friendship.

9. Enriquillo. The novel, of the same name, was written by Manuel de Jesús Galván (1834–1910) and published 1879-82. An English translation by Robert Graves appeared under the title *The Cross and the Sword* in 1954.

10. Victor Hugues, who led the French Revolution in Guadeloupe and ruled the island for four years. He abolished slavery, which was later reimposed by the Emperor Napoleon. Carpentier's novel is *El Siglo de las Luces* (1962), translated by John Sturrock as *Explosion in a Cathedral* (1963).

49 Literary ladies

1. Maria Nugent, wife of General George Nugent. Lady Nugent's *Journal* of her residence in Jamaica from 1801 to 1805 (fourth edition, 1966) is highly readable, as well as being an important historical source for the period.
2. Mary Prince. Her *History of Mary Prince, A West Indian Slave, related by herself* was first published in 1831.
3. *The Wonderful Adventures of Mrs Seacole in many lands,* first published in 1857. She was Mary Seacole.
4. Jean Rhys. The book, of course, was *Wide Sargasso Sea.* The author was born in Dominica as Ella Gwendolen Rees Williams.
5. The Dominican politician and journalist, Phyllis Shand Allfrey, author of *The Orchid House* (1953).
6. Jamaica Kincaid.
7. Zee Edgell. The novel is *Beka Lamb* (1982).
8. Olive Senior.
9. Grace Nichols.
10. Maryse Condé, who is the author of several other novels.

50 Author, author!

1f *Mother Poem* (1977) is the first of a trilogy of book-length poems by the Barbadian poet and historian, Kamau Brathwaite.

2g Taking the events of the Haitian Revolution as its starting point, the novel *The Kingdom of This World* (original title, *El Reino de este Mundo*, 1949), by the Cuban writer Alejo Carpentier, is a pioneering work in the style which has come to be known by the name he gave it – 'magical realism'.

3h *Stories written in exile* (Spanish title, *Cuentos Escritos en el Exilio*, 1962) is one of the best known literary works of Juan Bosch, former president of the Dominican Republic.

4b *Return to my Native Land* (*Cahier d'un retour au pays natal*; originally published 1939) is the most famous and influential work of the Martiniquan poet and politician Aimé Césaire, one of the leaders of the Négritude (black consciousness) movement in Francophone Africa and the Caribbean.

5i *In the Castle of My Skin* (1953) is the first and best known book of the Barbadian novelist George Lamming.

6c A multi-layered novel of unhappy love and the crippling psychological effects of colonialism, *Wide Sargasso Sea* (1966) is by the Dominican-born Jean Rhys.

7k *Another Life* (1973) is a long autobiographical poem by Derek Walcott, the St Lucian winner of the 1992 Nobel Prize for Literature.

8j *West Indies Ltd* (1934) is one of many collections of poems by Nicolás Guillén, recognised as the national poet of Cuba.

9e One of the best known Haitian novels, *Masters of the Dew* (originally published as *Gouverneurs de la Rosée* in 1944) is by Jacques Roumain.

10a Published in 1961, *A House for Mr Biswas*, which uses the author's Trinidadian Indian heritage as a basis for profound – and at times richly comic – reflection on the human condition, remains one of V.S.Naipaul's most popular novels.

11d *Black Shack Alley* (originally published as *La Rue Cases-Nègres* in 1950) is a novel by the Martiniquan writer Joseph Zobel. It has been made into an internationally successful film by the Martiniquan director Euzhan Palcy.

More about our illustrations

Most of our illustrations are related to one of the questions in the quiz in which they appear, or to the quiz as a whole. We didn't want to give too much away, so there are no captions with the pictures – but here are the details.

Quiz 1
View of the former House of Assembly building, Spanish Town, Jamaica, built in the mid-18th century. ©John Gilmore.

Quiz 2
Cloud forest on Mount Scenery, Saba, Netherlands Antilles. ©John Gilmore.

Quiz 3
Beach scene, Bequia, St Vincent and the Grenadines. ©Trip/D. Davis.

Quiz 4
Old waterwheel, still used to power cane-grinding machinery at River Antoine, Grenada. ©John Gilmore.

Quiz 5

1. The Pitons, St Lucia. ©CORBIS.
2. El Morro, Puerto Rico. ©CORBIS.
3. Columbus Lighthouse, Dominican Republic. ©John Gilmore.
4. Kaieteur Falls, Guyana. ©Travel Ink/Ian Brierley.
5. The Circus, Basseterre, St Kitts. ©Travel Ink/Roy Westlake.
6. Independence Arch and Parliament Buildings, Bridgetown, Barbados. ©Travel Ink/Geoff Clive.
7. New Kingston, Kingston, Jamaica. ©Trip/J. Highet.
8. St John's Cathedral, St John's, Antigua. ©CORBIS.
9. Punda waterfront, Willemstad, Curaçao. ©CORBIS.
10. Stollmeyer's Castle, Port of Spain, Trinidad and Tobago. ©CORBIS.

Quiz 6
View of Scarborough, Tobago. ©Trip/B. Turner.

Quiz 7
Caribbean flags (Gary Fielder, AC Design).

Quiz 8
Grass air-strip in the interior of Suriname. ©John Gilmore.

Quiz 9

Entrance to the fortress at Brimstone Hill, St Kitts. ©John Gilmore.

Quiz 10

View of part of St-Pierre, Martinique, a few days before the volcanic eruption of 1902. The volcanic cloud from the Montagne Pélée is clearly visible. (Contemporary postcard from the John Gilmore collection.)

Quiz 11
View of George Town, Cayman Islands. ©CORBIS

Quiz 12
National coat of arms of Grenada – note the tatou on the left. ©Grenada Board of Tourism.

Quiz 13
A Saba lizard (*Anolis sabanus*), found only on the five square miles of Saba, Netherlands Antilles. ©John Gilmore.

Quiz 14
Flamingos at Goto Lake, Bonaire, Netherlands Antilles. ©John Gilmore.

Quiz 15
Fishermen returning to shore, Grenada. ©John Gilmore.

Quiz 16
Harvesting coca pods, Trinidad. From an early 20th-century postcard (John Gilmore collection).

Quiz 17
Jamaican ackees being offered for sale. ©Trip/D. Saunders.

Quiz 18
Rum, sugar and limes. ©John Gilmore.

Quiz 19
Jamaican athlete, Merlene Ottey. ©Popperfoto.

Quiz 20
'An important match' – early 20th century postcard from Barbados (John Gilmore collection).

Quiz 21
1 Denyse Plummer. ©Star Publishing.
2 C. L. R. James. ©Serpents Tail.
3 Brian Lara. ©Popperfoto.
4 Bob Marley. ©CORBIS.
5 Maryse Condé. ©Vif Anderson.
6 Fidel Castro. ©Popperfoto.
7 Jean Rhys. ©Jean Rhys Co. Ltd.
8 Cheddi Jagan. ©www.jagan.org.
9 Dame Eugenia Charles. ©Popperfoto.
10 Michael Manley. ©CORBIS.

Quiz 22
(no picture)

Quiz 23
Imaginary portrait of Sam Sharpe, from the Jamaican $50 note. ©MELT.

Quiz 24
Lester Bird, Prime Minister of Antigua and Barbuda. ©John Gilmore.

Quiz 25
Sam Lord's Castle, Barbados, as it was in the early 20th century (postcard, John Gilmore collection).

Quiz 26
Dr Denzil Douglas, Prime Minister of St Kitts and Nevis. ©John Gilmore.

Quiz 27
Collage of Caribbean banknotes. ©MELT.

Quiz 28
From left to right:
1 Pre-Columbian Amerindian rock carving in Grenada. ©John Gilmore.
2 Pre-Columbian Amerindian rock carving in St Kitts. ©John Gilmore.
3 Present-day Amerindian village in Suriname. ©John Gilmore.

Quiz 29
King William IV of Great Britain. ©CORBIS

Quiz 30
View of Philipsburg, capital of St Maarten, Netherlands Antilles.
©John Gilmore.

Quiz 31
Olaudah Equiano, from the frontispiece to his autobiography, *The Interesting Narrative of the Life of Olaudah Equiano...* (first published 1789).
©The Bridgeman Art Library.

Quiz 32
View of the Cathedral and surrounding area, Fort de France, Martinique. ©Travel Ink/Roy Westlake.

Quiz 33
Queen Beatrix of the Netherlands (in pink and white dress) goes walkabout in Willemstad, Curaçao, capital of the Netherlands Antilles. ©John Gilmore.

Quiz 34
Left: Birthplace of Alexander Hamilton, Charlestown, Nevis (now the Nevis Museum). ©John Gilmore.
Right: Fort Oranje, Oranjestad, St Eustatius, Netherlands Antilles. ©John Gilmore.

Quiz 35
A celebration of the Hosay Festival in early 20th century Jamaica (from a postcard in the John Gilmore collection).

Quiz 36
Fields of young sugar-canes, Guadeloupe. ©John Gilmore.

Quiz 37
Crop Over Festival, Barbados. ©CORBIS

Quiz 38
Worshippers leaving St Paul's Anglican Church, Bridgetown, Barbados, after a Sunday morning service. ©John Gilmore.

Quiz 39
Cave Hill, Barbados, campus of the University of the West Indies. ©Virginia Foster.

Quiz 40
Cathedral of Santa María de la Encarnación, Santo Domingo, Dominican Republic. ©John Gilmore.

Quiz 41
Adapted from a painting by Aubrey Williams.

Quiz 42
Sparrow in concert.©Redferns.

Quiz 43
Tuk band in Barbados. ©CORBIS

Quiz 44
Small stone huts in Bonaire, Netherlands Antilles, built in the mid-19th century for the slaves who worked in the island's salt-pans. ©John Gilmore.

Quiz 45
Juvenile Green Monkey in gulley.©Julia Horrocks.

Quiz 46
Strolling minstrel, in a photographer's studio in Barbados, early 20th century (from a postcard in the John Gilmore collection).

Quiz 47
Collage of Caribbean newspapers. ©MELT.

Quiz 48
Modern restrike of 19th century pattern coin showing a representation of Henri Christophe, King of Haiti. The original was perhaps designed on the king's instructions, but this is uncertain and it may be a later concoction intended for sale to collectors. ©MELT.

Quiz 49
Guyanese author Grace Nichols. ©Gillian Cargill

Quiz 50
St Lucia's Nobel Prize winner, Derek Walcott. ©MELT.